Cherry Menlove

The HANDMADE HOME

First published in Great Britain in 2013
by Weidenfeld & Nicolson

1 3 5 7 9 10 8 6 4 2

To download the templates used in this book at full scale, please go to:
www.orionbooks.co.uk/handmadehome

A CIP catalogue record for this book is available from the British Library.

ISBN: 978 0 297 86651 0

Printed and bound in China

The Orion Publishing Group's policy is to use papers that are natural, renewable and recyclable and made from wood grown in sustainable forests. The logging and manufacturing processes are expected to conform to environmental regulations of the country of origin.

Publisher: Amanda Harris; Art Direction and design: Nikki Dupin; Editorial: Aruna Vasudevan and Nicola Crossley; Photographer: Keiko Oikawa; Illustrator: Kuo Kang Chen; Food stylist: Nikki Morgan; Proofreader: Laura Nickoll; Indexer: Elizabeth Wiggans; Consultant: Jodie Beth Wilson; Assistant: Cathy Whitby

Weidenfeld & Nicolson
Orion Publishing Group Ltd
Orion House
5 Upper Saint Martin's Lane
London, WC2H 9EA

An Hachette UK Company

www.orionbooks.co.uk

Cherry Menlove

The HANDMADE HOME

Inspirational craft, food and flowers

Cherry Menlove started her career by creating a hugely successful blog, writing about the subject she loves most – her home and garden. Her website (www.cherrymenlove.com) currently has about 2.4 million hits a year. Cherry also writes for *Sainsbury's Magazine* and she regularly contributes to *Easy Living* magazine online. The classes at her baking school 'Picket Fence Baking, feel good baking' are regularly sold out and her video tutorials reach a global audience. She is married with twins.

Emma Freud on Cherry Menlove: five things you *should* know…

1. She has the best name of anyone in the world. Apart from Immodesty Blaize, Gina Lollobrigida and Pussy Galore, obviously.

2. This is how we met. One dinnertime last year, I googled 'great recipe for slow-cooked lamb' and came across Cherry's incredible concoction. It involved nearly a full bottle of maple syrup. I knew then that we were going to be friends. We tweeted each other for about a year after that. Then one day she arrived at my house (I had invited her; she wasn't stalking or anything) with a pot of homemade cherry jam, some baked Madeleines and a huge sweetcorn from her vegetable patch. All nestled in a white trug that had been made by her handsome dad. By the time she had walked through the door, I was already a bit in love with her.

3. The thing about Cherry is that she has a gently old-fashioned, and at the same time incredibly modern, attitude to her life. She has an unashamed, almost embarrassing passion for her house, her garden, her children, her husband, her friends, her village and the countryside. It isn't fashionable and isn't feminist, but it strikes me as being very contemporary. Although she's had a rocking professional career, it's her home that she's made the centre of her world. She's happy but not smug. She's energetic but not annoying. She's creative but not perfect. She loves the land in a way that only a girl who has lived most of her life in town could love it. It's not a given, it's a privilege, and her zest for it has made me rethink my life and my environment. She cherishes her house and treasures it – not because it's beautiful (which it is), but because it's the engine of her life. And, this book isn't about being wealthy or a bit *Country Living*, it's about a sparklingly modern girl, who is proud to invest her time and her love in nurturing her domestic world.

4. Imagine a quirky, pretty, funky mash-up between Mrs Beeton, Martha Stewart, Hugh Fearnley-Whittingstall and a saucy French maid: Cherry is that love child.

5. Her mince pies are the single most delicious objects known to humankind.

HELLO! MY NAME IS CHERRY AND THIS IS MY FIRST BOOK. I'm thrilled to have written about a subject that I believe in and love with all my heart: the home. The following 12 chapters celebrate special and everyday occasions that crop up over one year – from Valentine's Day and a bank holiday barbeque to Halloween, a winter weekend with friends and Christmas.

I am extremely passionate about the home and have always dreamed of having a home where the door is always open, the fridge always full and the beds always comfortable. I have worked very hard to make this dream a reality and although I am self-taught in the ways of cooking, baking and crafting, I have been able to draw on age-old methods passed down to me by my parents and grandparents. I wanted to share all this and my absolute joy with all things home and garden with other people – and that is what prompted me to set up my website in the first place.

Since I began writing my blog, I have been lucky enough to attract an audience who love their homes as much as I do. I truly believe that you can find the strength to deal with whatever life throws at you, if your home is working properly and is giving you back what you deserve.

While writing this book, I discovered this first-hand. My husband, Robert, was diagnosed with leukaemia and I decided it was important to make sure that my baby twins had a safe, loving and beautiful home. I wanted to make sure that no matter what, they would always know the importance of home to their parents and how, in times of deep trouble, it can provide refuge and great strength. I'm now overjoyed to say that my husband, and home, have made it through this toughest of tests.

ENJOY THE BOOK.
ALL MY LOVE,

Cherry
x

HOW TO USE
THIS BOOK

This book is arranged by section: recipes are found in **From the kitchen**; crafts in **From the craft room**; advice on growing flowers, fruit and vegetables in **From the garden** and how to set up the occasion in **From the home**.

KEY TO ICONS IN THE TEXT:

 food suitable for making in advance

 suitable for a present

 food suitable for freezing

 Cherry's tip/suitable for children

 Cherry's tip

Valentine's Day

IT'S FEBRUARY, Christmas is well and truly over, the New Year has begun in earnest and the time is right for one of the first celebrations of the year. Personally I'm very grateful that Valentine's Day falls in the middle of February. It can be a dark month, which offers few signs of spring, and I love the fact that there is something to plan for and celebrate.

I also like Valentine's Day because it gives you permission to celebrate those you love for the day. It certainly doesn't need to be limited to romantic partners. What about your best friend, workmates, siblings, grandparents or children? I say they all deserve a day when they are spoilt and have love lavished upon them. Valentine's Day shouldn't be exclusively for smoochy young couples.

In this chapter you'll find a simple craft for my personal favourite treat, breakfast in bed, along with some great recipes in case you choose to bestow this gift upon someone special. Anyone who bestows it on me is a friend for life, by the way. I have no problem finding you in my bedroom if you're carrying a tray with my Gruyère and Tarragon Breakfast Omelette on it, no matter who you are!

There are also some lovely gift ideas and tips on how to decorate your table and home so that it's ready for a Valentine's Day party. It's February, we took January off to recover, so now is the time to get our celebratory groove back.

I've included two crafts in this chapter. The tray cover is pretty, but also very practical. The Valentine's card and envelope simply beats a shop-bought card, hands down – and I've also been able to put the heart template to other uses (*see pages 18 and 30*).

Valentine's Tray Cover

YOU WILL NEED:

- Tray (29cm x 47cm)
- Fabric (100cm x 50cm)
- Measuring tape
- Scissors
- Heatproof filling, such as Insul Bright
- Pins
- Sewing machine
- Sewing cotton
- Roll of parchment paper
- Pencil
- 2m bias binding

NOTE: For a smaller or bigger tray, please adjust the sizes accordingly.

TO MAKE THE TRAY LINER

1. Cut the fabric into 2 pieces, each measuring 28cm x 46cm (this ensures it fits snugly inside the tray). Cut the heatproof filling to the same size. Place one of the pieces of fabric face down on a flat surface and lay the heatproof filling on top. Put the other piece of fabric face up on top. Ensure all the edges line up exactly. Pin and sew all 3 layers together 5mm from the edge (*see image 1*).

2. Cut 3 strips of parchment paper, measuring 9cm x 46cm. Draw a row of joined-up hearts along each strip. Pin the strips, one above the other, onto the top layer of fabric (*see image 2*).

3. Following the pattern of the heart shapes, sew them onto the fabric. Remove the pins and carefully tear the paper free of the stitches (*see image 3*).

1

2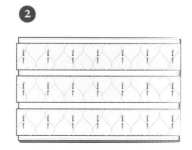

3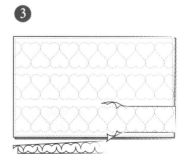

TO ATTACH THE BINDING

4. Start in the middle of an edge of the tray liner and pin the bias binding all the way around. Leave 5cm of extra binding unpinned at each end. To create neat corners, pinch the binding at the corner edge and then neatly fold back inwards (*see image 4*). Sew in place.

5. To sew the 2 ends of binding together, pin the binding at the point where the 2 lengths meet (*see image 5*).

6. Turn the 2 ends so that they are face to face and at right angles to each other. Sew diagonally across from left to right (*see image 6*).

7. Trim off the excess binding (*see image 7*) and turn the right way out. Finish by pinning and sewing the remaining part of binding in place.

Valentine's Card and Envelope

YOU WILL NEED:

Envelope

- Fabric (25cm x 25cm)
- Pins
- Sewing machine
- Sewing cotton
- Iron
- Fabric pencil
- Needle
- 1 skein embroidery thread

Card

- Card (30cm x 15cm)
- A4 sheet tracing paper
- Fabric (11cm x 11cm)
- Scissors (paper/fabric)
- Sewing machine
- Sewing cotton

TO MAKE THE ENVELOPE

1. Take the fabric square and lay it pattern-side down on a flat surface in the shape of a diamond (*see image 1, right*). Fold and pin a double hem (1cm per hem) along 2 adjoining sides and sew neatly in place.

2. Turn the fabric over so that it is pattern-side up. Take a half-hemmed corner and the unhemmed corner and place face to face (thereby folding the fabric in half; *see image 2, right*). Pin and sew 5mm from the unhemmed edge.

3. Bring the other half-hemmed corner to the unhemmed corner that has just been sewn and place face to face (*see image 3, right*). Pin and sew the openings these create, 5mm from the edge.

4. Turn the right way out and iron flat (*see image 4, right*).

5. Use the fabric pencil to write a word or message on the front of the envelope. Sew over the lettering with embroidery thread in a running stitch (*see image 5, right*).

TO MAKE THE CARD

6. Lay the card down landscape on a flat surface. Fold the longer length in half to create a 15cm x 15cm square.

7. Place the tracing paper over the heart (*left*) and draw around it. Carefully cut it out and lay it on the back of the fabric. Trace around it and cut the heart out.

8. Carefully position the heart on the front of the card and hold in place. Following the outline of the heart, double stitch in place 3–5mm from the edge of the material (*see image 6, right*).

TEMPLATE FOR
HEART

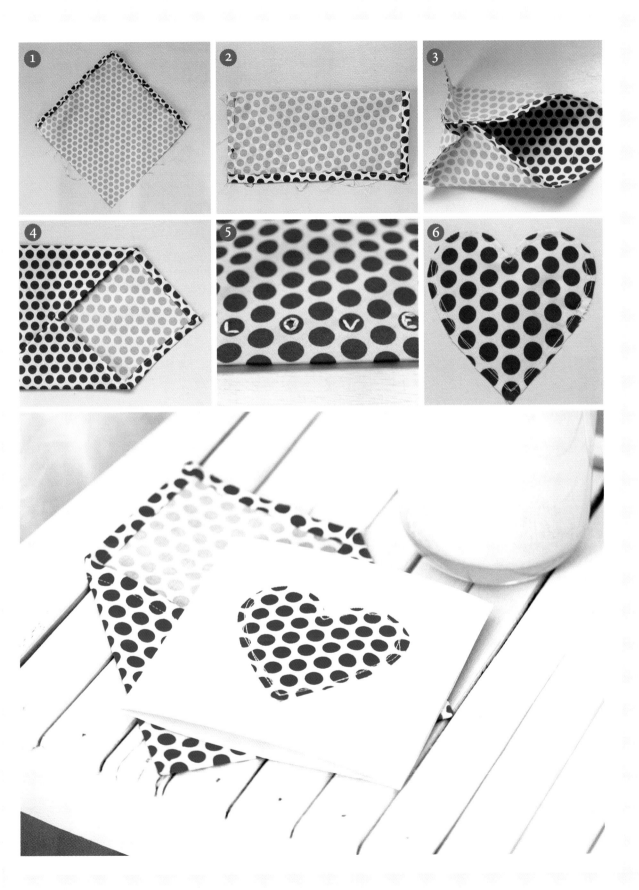

If you are making breakfast in bed for another person it is important to know what they like to eat. Robert, for instance, absolutely loves French toast served up with crispy bacon and the sweetest maple syrup. I know when I serve that up he'll scoff the lot and ask for more. In addition to this, as it is Valentine's Day, I make a herby omelette and some special sweetheart biscuits and marshmallows. The latter can be tricky to get just right and take concentration, but the gentle rose flavouring makes them an absolute joy.

French Toast with Bacon and Maple Syrup

SERVES: 2

INGREDIENTS
2 thick slices white
    farmhouse bread
2 large eggs
2 tbsp double cream
½ tsp ground cinnamon
½ tsp ground nutmeg
4 slices smoked
    streaky bacon
20g unsalted butter
Icing sugar, for dusting
2 tbsp maple syrup,
    for serving

Take 2 slices of bread and place them side by side in a baking dish.

In a medium-sized bowl whisk together the eggs, cream, cinnamon and nutmeg until fully combined. Pour the mixture over the bread, making sure the slices are evenly coated. Leave to soak for 2–3 minutes.

Place the bacon under a very hot grill and cook until crispy, turning twice.

In a large non-stick frying pan, over a low heat, gently heat the butter until melted. Fry the soaked bread for 2–3 minutes on each side, until brown and slightly crispy.

Place the French toast onto a warm serving plate. Cut diagonally in half and dust lightly with icing sugar.

Serve with the crispy bacon and drizzled maple syrup.

Gruyère and Tarragon Breakfast Omelette

SERVES: 1–2

INGREDIENTS

4 large eggs
1 tbsp double cream
1 heaped tbsp finely chopped
    fresh tarragon
Sea salt
Ground black pepper
20g unsalted butter
5 heaped tbsp grated
    Gruyère cheese

In a large bowl, whisk together the egg, cream and tarragon until pale and fluffy. Season to taste with salt and pepper.

In a non-stick frying pan, over a medium heat, gently heat the butter. Tilt the pan to coat the surface evenly. Pour the egg mixture into the pan, making sure that the bottom of the pan is covered. Fry for 3–4 minutes, or until the mixture is almost set.

Sprinkle the grated cheese into the centre of the omelette and flip one side over so that it just covers the cheese. Fold the other side over so that it seals the omelette.

Carefully flip the omelette once and then fry for 2–3 minutes more until golden.

Serve on a warm plate.

TIP Another great combination is red pepper and finely cubed feta cheese, topped with chopped coriander. I ate these for weeks after my twins were born.

Valentine Sweethearts

These homemade vanilla and almond Valentine biscuits make a great gift. They look impressive piled high on a cake stand or just wrapped up simply in cellophane with a pretty bow.

MAKES: 16 biscuits

INGREDIENTS

Biscuits
200g unsalted butter, softened
200g caster sugar
1 large egg, beaten
400g plain flour, plus a little extra for dusting
½ tsp vanilla extract
½ tsp almond extract

Decoration
5–6 tbsp water
600g icing sugar, sifted
1–2 drops rose food colouring
1–2 drops pink food colouring (or contrasting colours of your choice)

SPECIAL EQUIPMENT
Heart-shaped 10cm cookie, cutter; piping bag with #2 nozzle

Preheat the oven to 180°C/Gas 4. Line a baking tray with parchment paper. Set aside.

Use a free-standing mixer with a paddle attachment to mix the butter and sugar together until just combined. Beat the egg into the mixture; sift in the flour and add in the drops of vanilla and almond extract. On a slow speed, mix all of the ingredients until they come together to form a soft dough ball; when the dough comes away from the bowl's sides it is ready. Wrap the dough in cling film and chill for 30 minutes.

Remove the dough from the fridge and sprinkle a clean work surface with flour. Roll the dough out to a thickness of 5mm. Use the cookie cutter to cut out 16 heart shapes.

Place the hearts onto the lined baking tray, making sure they are evenly spaced out. Put in the fridge to chill for 30 minutes.

Place the biscuits in the preheated oven for 6–8 minutes, or until they are cream in colour. Remove the biscuits from the oven and leave to cool on the baking tray before decorating.

To make the decoration, place 2 tablespoons of water in the bowl of a free-standing mixer with the whisk attachment, and sift in 200g of the icing sugar. Whisk together for 1–2 minutes. Sift in another 200g of icing sugar, along with 1–2 tablespoons of water and a few drops of rose food colouring (or the colouring of your choice).

Whisk on a high speed for about 4–6 minutes, or until the mixture forms straight peaks. If the mixture is too runny, add a little more icing sugar and if it becomes too stiff, add some more water a drop at a time.

Spoon about 4 tablespoons of icing into the piping bag. Then, carefully trace an icing line around the outer edge of the heart biscuit.

Return any icing to the bowl and add more water, a drop at a time. Whisk the icing again until it turns slightly runny in consistency, but is not watery.

Use a teaspoon to drizzle the icing into the middle of each of the biscuits and gently spread the icing around so that it covers the surface of the biscuit evenly and smoothly. The piping around the edge should prevent the icing from running over the edges. Leave for 3 hours to let the icing set.

In the clean bowl of the mixer, on a high speed, whisk together the last 200g of icing sugar, 2 tablespoons of water and 1–2 drops of pink food colouring for 3–4 minutes, or until the icing forms straight peaks.

Spoon the icing into the piping bag. Carefully pipe dots all the way around the edge of each iced biscuit.

Strawberry Rose Marshmallows

MAKES: 30

INGREDIENTS
200g fresh strawberries
335ml cold water
10 x fine leaf gelatine sheets
1 vanilla pod
250ml Karo Light corn syrup
700g caster sugar
1 tbsp Le Sirop de
    Monin Rose
50g icing sugar, sifted, plus
    extra for dusting
50g cornflour

SPECIAL EQUIPMENT
Baking tray (25cm x 30cm);
parchment paper; cooking
thermometer

Line the baking tray with the parchment paper. Put to one side.

Wash and hull the strawberries. Slice in half and add to a medium-sized saucepan along with 30ml of water. Gently heat the strawberries for about 5–7 minutes, until they are pulp-like in consistency, then remove from the heat.

Use a hand-held blender to purèe the strawberries. Pass through a sieve and pour the pulp into the bowl of a free-standing mixer.

Place the gelatine leaves in a separate bowl and cover with cold water; leave for 5 minutes. Using a sharp knife, split the vanilla pod, scrape out the seeds and add the seeds to the strawberry pulp. Drain the gelatine leaves, squeezing out any excess water and add to the purèe, along with 125ml of fresh cold water. Set the bowl to one side.

In a large saucepan, heat the remaining 180ml of cold water, corn syrup and sugar and stir until combined. Use the thermometer to gauge the temperature. It is ready when the syrup has reached a temperature of 115°C.

Take the saucepan off the heat and carefully pour the syrup into the purèe mix. Add the rose syrup and whisk in a free-standing mixer at a low/medium speed. As the mixture starts to stiffen, increase to a medium/fast speed. It should turn a light pink colour, thicken and become shiny. It is ready when it drips slowly off the whisk. This should take 10 –20 minutes.

Pour the marshmallow mixture onto the lined baking tray and chill overnight.

In a medium-sized bowl combine the sifted icing sugar and cornflour. Remove the marshmallow from the fridge and turn it out onto a large cutting board dusted with icing sugar.

Slowly peel back the parchment paper, dusting with icing sugar-cornflour mixture as you go. Use a large sharp knife to cut the marshmallows into 30 squares, each measuring 5cm x 5cm. Store in the fridge until ready to serve.

Spring is almost here and the garden remains cold, but even though it all looks rather barren outside, there are some flashes of colour perfect for use on Valentine's Day. This colour comes from plants such as hebe, heather, rosemary and bay. If you have any of these plants in your garden, that makes it much easier and far cheaper to put a seasonal bouquet together.

Once you've selected, picked and put together a small bunch from these plants, it's easy to make them look pretty. All you need to do is tie the ends together with raffia or bakers' twine and place your bouquet onto a plate on your breakfast tray or separate it out into a few glass bottles to spread around your Valentine's table. Equally, you can just give your loved one the whole bunch to keep.

Of course, depending on the winter we are having, daffodils, ranunculus and narcissus may have also made their appearance in the garden. In which case, you can also take advantage of these flowers, either cut or in small pots, planted especially for Valentine's Day.

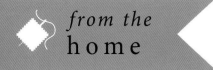

Decorating *your* Valentine's Table

Although I have focused on breakfast in this chapter, if you have invited your friends and family around to your home for a Valentine's Day celebration of some kind, then you may want to create a special table.

My Valentine's table is made up of bright colours, sweet confectionary and creamy chocolate, all topped off with some fabulous Valentine's decorations.

A FEW TIPS

- Create a tree by using seasonal branches of twisted hazel and a variety of pussy willow, all stuck into oasis foam at the bottom of a red jug.

- Use the template on page 18 to trace some simple heart shapes onto pieces of felt. Attach some ribbon or string and hang them from the trees (*see top photo, right*). The hearts are lightweight and can also be reused for birthday decorations or hung on a Christmas tree.

- An old trick for displaying sweets is to place a liqueur glass onto an upended espresso cup and fill it with chocolate hearts. It is easy to adapt this idea to create great individual table settings for a supper party. Simply add a name card and you're all set. The addition of specially created menu wraps (*see page 82*) can also be a lovely detail.

- Place small lollipops in bud vases. Just remember to add some oasis foam to the bottom of the vase if you're having trouble making them stand up straight.

Mother's Day

AHH MY MUM. As a very small child I remember her as a striking woman with jet-black hair and nails that were always painted. As a teen I recall this incredibly creative, energetic person who took up jogging one day and worked her way through several half marathons with an admirable nonchalance. She has remained energetic and morphed into a wonderful granny to her grandchildren. They love days out with her, and the years she worked as a teacher are paying great dividends in their lives.

My mum, like most mothers (myself included), likes nothing more than good food, good wine and her family around her. So the recipes, crafts and tips in this chapter don't have to be exclusive to your own mother. You can recreate this feast for any other mummy you know. Mummies like nothing more than time off, so to be cooked for, baked for and presented with a spread that celebrates them as a person as well as being unashamedly flowery and feminine is something they won't forget in a hurry.

I'm dedicating this chapter to all the mothers and 'mother' figures in people's lives. Without you we are nothing, and we love you.

I've chosen an heirloom craft for this chapter. The appliqué is fairly time consuming, but is a really nice way of giving someone a gift with a special message.

STEP *by* **STEP**

A 'Home Sweet Home' Appliqué

YOU WILL NEED:

- Assorted fabric, ribbon and ric–rac for house/garden
- Measuring tape
- Scissors (paper/fabric)
- Pins
- Needle
- Sewing cotton
- Fabric for background (50cm x 50cm)
- Computer and printer
- 13 x A4 sheets paper
- Pencil
- Stiff card (28cm x 35cm)
- Bamboo wadding (50cm x 50cm)
- Craft glue
- Picture frame

TO CREATE THE MAIN BODY OF THE HOUSE

1. Select and cut out a piece of fabric for the house front, measuring 15cm (h) x 12cm (w). From a contrasting piece, cut out 5 shapes for the windows, each measuring 3.5cm (h) x 2.5cm (w). From another piece, cut out a strip measuring 5cm (h) x 3cm (w) for the door. Lay the front of the house on a flat surface and pin 3 window pieces in a row at the top; line the door up with the middle window. Pin the 2 remaining windows in place, either side of the door. Sew into place using a small running stitch (*see image 1, right*).

TO FINISH THE HOUSE AND GARDEN

2. Take the background fabric square and cut out a piece, measuring 45cm (h) x 38cm (w). This measurement includes 5cm extra fabric per side for framing. Select a piece of fabric and cut out a slanted roof-shaped piece measuring 6cm (h) x 16cm (w: base) x 12cm (w: top); a strip of fabric for the garden, measuring 4cm (h) x 28cm (w); and 2 circles for the tops of the trees, each 5cm in diameter. Cut a 23cm length of patterned ribbon for the garden flowers and another 2 x 10cm lengths of green ric-rac for the tree trunks.

3. Assemble the house and garden by pinning the pieces into place onto the background fabric. Handstitch in place using a running stitch (*see image 2, right*).

TO CREATE THE MESSAGE

4. Use a computer to type out the words 'Home Sweet Home' (font 'American Typewriter'; point size 120). Print the letters and cut them out. Lay the letters face down on the back of a contrasting piece of fabric. Draw around the edges of the letters in pencil and cut them out. Position the letters in order, one word per line, above the fabric house appliqué. Pin and sew into place (*see image 3*).

TO FINISH AND FRAME

5. Once all the pieces are in place, take the stiff card and place it behind the appliqué. To give it extra padding, place the wadding between the fabric and card (*see image 4*). Make sure everything is centred before gluing the excess fabric onto the card back. Then frame.

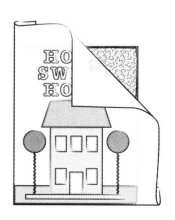

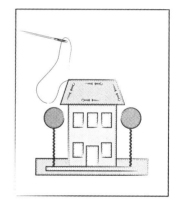

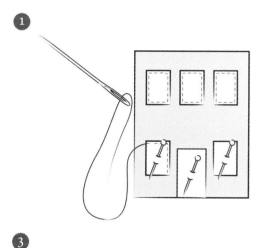

from the
kitchen

My mum loves the following dishes. She enjoys fresh ingredients and the fact that the dishes are perfect for a light spring lunch before we go out shopping or for a walk. The added advantage is that most of the recipes are easy to make and can be prepared in advance.

Pea and Mint Soup

SERVES: 4

INGREDIENTS
1 medium-sized waxy
   potato, cubed
75g unsalted butter
5 spring onions, chopped
600ml vegetable stock
500g fresh green peas
25g fresh mint, leaves only
600ml full-fat milk
¼ tsp sea salt
¼ tsp ground black pepper

In a large pan, over a high heat, cook the cubed potato in water until softened. Drain and set to one side.

In a large frying pan, melt the butter over a low heat, and cook the spring onions for 5–7 minutes, until softened.

Use the large pan to heat the vegetable stock, peas, mint and milk. Add in the cooked potato and season with salt and pepper to taste. Stir the soup and bring to boiling point.

Turn the heat right down and allow the soup to simmer for 30 minutes. Stir occasionally, skimming off any froth with a spoon.

Remove from heat. Pour into the bowl of a free-standing mixer or use a hand-held blender to blend until smooth.

Ladle the soup into serving bowls.

Serving suggestion: Drizzle a circle of crème fraîche onto each serving of soup. Garnish with pea shoots.

TIP Double the quantity and freeze any leftovers. This can then be taken out of the freezer and reheated for a quick, fuss-free lunch.

Monkfish and Chorizo Fishcakes
with Mustard Mayonnaise

MAKES: 6
SERVES: 1 (starter); 2 (main)

INGREDIENTS

Fishcakes

2 medium-sized waxy
   potatoes, cubed
180g monkfish
2 tbsp groundnut oil
75g finely chopped shallots
1 tbsp capers, chopped
100g chorizo, chopped into
   small pieces
100g white breadcrumbs
15g flat-leaf parsley,
   finely chopped
Sea salt
½ tsp ground black pepper
1 large egg

Mustard mayonnaise

1 large egg yolk
1 tsp Dijon mustard
½ tsp mustard powder
Salt
Ground white pepper
275ml sunflower oil

In a medium-sized saucepan, bring 500ml of salted water to the boil. Add the cubed potatoes and cook until soft. Drain and leave to cool.

While the potatoes are boiling, poach the monkfish for 15–18 minutes in enough preboiled water to cover it. Gently fry the shallots in 1 tablespoon of oil for 5 minutes, until they soften. Put the potatoes and shallots in a large bowl. Add the capers, chorizo and breadcrumbs and use your hands to mix the ingredients until fully combined.

Remove the poached fish from the heat and drain off any excess liquid. Cut into small cubes, then add to the potato mixture, along with chopped parsley and salt and pepper to taste.

In a small bowl, beat the egg before adding to the fishcake mix. Use clean hands to mix the ingredients together. Then divide the mixture equally and shape into 6 patties.

In a non-stick frying pan, heat 1 tablespoon of oil until hot and slide in the patties. Cook over a medium heat, allowing 5 minutes per side, or until the outsides are brown but not burnt.

To make the mustard mayonnaise, use a hand-held blender to mix together the egg yolk, mustard and the mustard powder in a large jug. Season with salt and pepper and blend on a high speed until all the ingredients are fully combined. On a slow speed, drizzle the oil into the jug. Mix until the liquid begins to emulsify and thicken. Once the mayonnaise has thickened to the point where it makes soft peaks, add more seasoning if necessary. This will keep for 2 days if stored in an airtight container in the fridge.

Serving suggestion: Place the fishcakes on individual plates with a handful of fresh pea shoots and a wedge of lime. Serve the mustard mayonnaise on the side.

TIP   For an alternative to monkfish, substitute with salmon or cod.

A *Very* Berry Jelly

This pretty jelly is a light and refreshing end to the lunch. With a tiny bit of adaptation, it can also make a great children's dessert.

SERVES: 6

INGREDIENTS
9 x fine leaf gelatine sheets
800ml cold water
100g caster sugar
3 tbsp Le Sirop de Monin
    fraise (strawberry)
3 tbsp Crème de Fraise
    des Bois
200ml prosecco
200g fresh strawberries,
washed, hulled and
    quartered
200g fresh raspberries,
    washed

Soak the gelatine leaves in a bowl of cold water for 4–5 minutes, until they swell. Remove the leaves from the bowl and squeeze out any excess water.

In a saucepan, heat 800ml of water over a low heat. Drop in the gelatine; add sugar and the strawberry syrup and strawberry liqueur. Stir for about 5–6 minutes, but do not let the mixture come to the boil.

Transfer the liquid into a large pouring jug. Add the prosecco and stir gently, allowing for the bubbles to settle.

Pour the jelly mixture evenly into 6 clean dessert bowls. Wash the fruit and cut the strawberries into small pieces, but leave the raspberries whole. Divide the fruit evenly between 6 bowls. Chill in the fridge until the jellies have set (a minimum of 4–5 hours, but overnight is best).

Serving suggestion: Decorate with tiny sprigs of fresh mint.

TIP Leave out the alcohol to make this suitable for children.

Flowers for a Lovely Day

My mum loves flowers. She doesn't grow a huge amount herself, preferring, instead, to relax in her garden as opposed to actually digging in it – perhaps a habit I should adopt from her. She does love to be given flowers though and I like to oblige as much as possible. Here's what I do.

Flowers are often expensive, particularly during those 'occasion' times of year, when florists and shops are likely to hike up prices and your choice may seem limited. So, if you aren't able to grow them yourself buy the best bunch you can afford and split it up.

By putting small groups of flowers in pretty receptacles (and I've even used a metal tea caddy before), you can spread the joy. For flower vases, I prefer to use clear glass medicine bottles, vintage if you can find them, but a glass jar or a bunch of flowers wrapped around a gift can be equally as impressive.

IF YOU DO GROW FLOWERS, HERE ARE A FEW OF MY FAVOURITES

- **HYACINTHS:** One head will fill a room with the flower's distinctive syrupy scent.

- **RANUNCULUS:** Rather iconic nowadays, although they are not heavily scented these blousy beauties will drape gently over a vase. Your mum will fall in love with them.

- **NARCISSUS OR DAFFODIL:** These can be started from bulb in a pretty pot or tin just a few weeks prior to Mother's Day. These flowers also make a perfect gift. Their smell is divine.

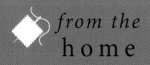

My Mother's Day Table

As we are not taking my mum out to lunch, I want to make that extra effort with the table. I'm hugely inspired by the French country way of decorating; the fabulous art of mixing shabby and distressed with delicate and feminine. The two styles complement each other so well and by using a soft palette of lilacs, pinks, yellows and greens, it is gentle but not too sugary. You can't really get a more lovely aesthetic, or one more suited to this occasion.

Everyday house and garden objects can be used in the design. For example, I use a rather rickety small white stepladder for my dessert trolley. I place the jelly bowls out on the steps and serve them from there. For special occassions, such as garden parties, I might bring the ladder to the table, as a centrepiece, to add a bit of outdoor charm. And, of course, this is where that bouquet of flowers that I have spilt up into bottles really comes into its own. If any place looks a bit neglected or bare, such as the steps, just pop a bottled flower or two in place – and voilà, you have a beautiful fragrant space.

Placing a narrow wooden garden crate upside down on the table top (*see photo, right*) creates a makeshift trivet. This can be decorated by placing a stack of pretty china cake plates and a soft posy of dried hydrangea heads on top. I have to say this is what I love most about decorating in this style: the simple but effective juxtaposition of a rustic wooden crate with a few delicate plates and petals. A decorative marriage made in heaven and a look that works particularly well in spring.

An Easter Picnic

THERE ARE FEW THINGS that make me happier than a warm Easter weekend, primarily because it means I can have a picnic. I love picnics and actively look forward to the time that I can lie down on the grass and stare up at the sun. Easter is usually the first opportunity to do this in the year, due to the weather.

There's something so delicious about being able to call up friends and arrange to meet them outside for a bite to eat on the nearest patch of grass, whether it be your garden, a nearby park or common. A picnic can be ever so glamorous, if you know what to pack and it's much easier to put together than you might think.

In the following pages, I give you some tips on how to create an Easter picnic. There are recipes for some dishes that are especially good when eaten al fresco, such as a rosemary and olive focaccia bread that makes use of the herb pots in my kitchen, a lovely salad and a tart or two. I also tell you how to make a 'Laying on the Lawn' quilt that is not only a perfect picnic blanket, but can also be kept as an heirloom. And Easter, of course, wouldn't be Easter without eggs of some description, so you'll find instructions on how to make some decorative fabric eggs (*see photo, right*).

The most helpful advice I can give you for a picnic of this kind is do as much as you can in advance. Then, just add in a little bit of sunshine and you're set … go picnic!

from the
craft room

My 'Laying on the Lawn' quilt is probably the largest craft in this book. It may take time to complete, but can be kept for years. I like the idea that one day my kids might use it with their own children.

STEP *by* **STEP**

'Laying on the Lawn' Quilt

YOU WILL NEED:

- Quilting fabric for front/back sections (9m x 1.14m)
- Measuring tape
- Rotary cutter
- Cutting mat (60cm x 45cm)
- Scissors (paper/fabric)
- Pins
- Sewing cotton
- Sewing machine
- Computer and printer
- 15 x A4 sheets paper
- Fabric for lettering (1m x 1m)
- Pencil
- Contrasting quilting fabric for border (2.5m x 1.14m)
- Iron and ironing board
- Bamboo wadding (2.5m x 2.5m)

You need a large open space to make this quilt so, if you have access to an outdoor space, why not work in the sunshine?

TO MAKE THE MAIN FRONT AND BACK SECTIONS

1. Take the fabric for the front and back sections and use the rotary cutter and mat (or scissors) to cut out 4 pieces (2 for the front; 2 for the back), each measuring 218cm (l) x 110cm (w). Pin 2 of the front pieces lengthways face to face. Sew together 1cm from the edge of the fabric. Repeat the process for the back, using the 2 other pieces.

TO CREATE THE LETTERING

2. On a computer, type out the words 'Laying on the Lawn' (font Baskerville Semibold; point size 775), using a separate page per letter. Print and carefully cut out each letter. Pin them face down onto the reverse of the 1m x 1m fabric square. Draw and cut each letter out. Lay the lettering out on the front section of the quilt and pin into place. Set the sewing machine to a zigzag stitch approximately 5mm wide. Sew around the edge of each letter.

TO CREATE THE BORDER AND CORNERS

3. Cut the border fabric into 4 strips, each measuring 250cm (l) x 28cm (w). Fold each strip in half widthways and iron along the fold to create a border piece 14cm wide. Lay the front section face up on the floor. Take the border strips and place one along each edge of the front section, open edges facing inwards. To create the stitching allowance, make sure that the front section of the quilt overlaps each border strip by 1cm. Pin the strips to the front section of the quilt along one of the open edges. The 2cm of excess fabric at each end of the border pieces are for hemming later (see image 1).

4. Draw a line in pencil from the outer tip to the inner corner of one half of the folded fabric. This will be the stitching line. Repeat on the other half of the border strip (see image 2).

5. Draw a second parallel line running 1.5cm from the stitching line on both halves of the fabric. This will be the cutting line and it will be closer to the edge of the fabric (see image 3). Repeat this step, drawing the stitching and cutting line on the other 3 corners of the border fabric. Unpin the border strips from the front section of the quilt. Cut along the 2 cutting lines (the outer lines) and discard the excess fabric (see image 4). Place 2 border strips face to face and pin together. To create a border corner, sew along the 2 stitching lines. Repeat with the remaining corners to create a square border frame (see image 5).

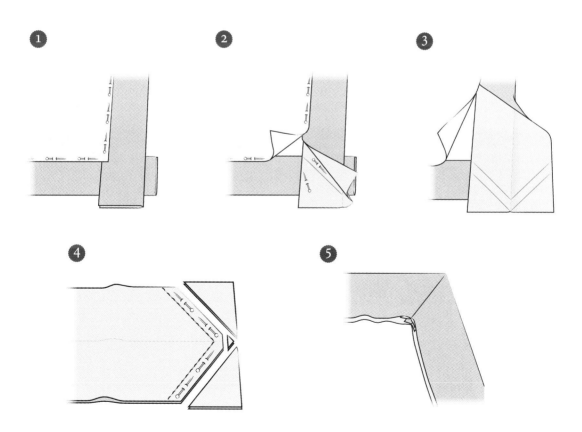

TO ATTACH THE BORDER TO THE FRONT SECTION

6. Lay the front section of the quilt on the floor so that the lettering is face up. Turn the border frame inside out. Pin the lower half of the border frame face to face along the top edge of the front section of the quilt. Allowing for a 1cm hem (*see image 6, right*). Continue to pin the border in this way along the other 3 edges of the front section. Once the border frame has been sewn in place, fold the border back over right side out.

TO MEASURE THE WADDING

7. Lay the quilt face down on the floor. Tuck the wadding up into the border corners and along all 4 border edges. It should fit snugly inside the edges of the border frame and lie flat. Trim off any excess as bamboo wadding has a lot of give (*see image 7, right*).

TO ATTACH THE BACK SECTION

8. Remove the wadding and turn the quilt inside out. Pin the back section of the quilt face down and face to face to the remaining border edge (*see image 8, right*), allowing for a 1cm hem. To enable the wadding to be inserted, leave a 1m side section unpinned. Sew the back section of the quilt in place. Turn the quilt the right way out and lay flat. Push the wadding into the quilt through the open section, making sure it is smooth, flat and fills all 4 corners properly.

TO SECURE THE WADDING AND CLOSE THE BORDER GAP

9. Lay the quilt face up on the floor. Pin all 3 layers of the quilt together 1cm in from the outer edge of the border. To secure the layers together, it is necessary to pin along the top of the seams, where the front and back sections of the quilt meet the border (*see image 9, right*).

10. To pin the open 1m section of the quilt closed, fold the border fabric over by 5mm and pin onto the back section of the quilt by following the existing border seam.

11. Using the pins as a guide, sew along the quilt, thus securing the wadding in place. At the gap, sew 2mm onto the border to close up the opening. Ensure the front and back section seams line up. Sew along the outer edge of the border using the pins as a guide.

12. Lay the quilt face up on the floor. Avoiding the lettering, pin 5 evenly spaced lines horizontally across the quilt from one border seam to the opposite border seam. Sew along the pins to create the quilting effect (*see image 10, right*). This also further secures the wadding, preventing it from moving around and resulting in an uneven finish.

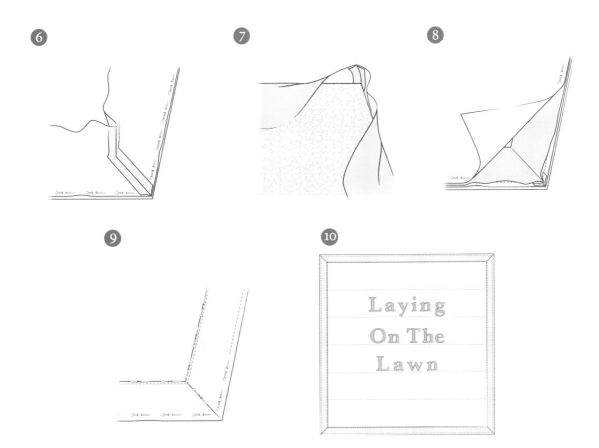

6 **7** **8**

9 **10**

Laying
On The
Lawn

STEP by STEP

Fabric Easter Eggs

Easter wouldn't be complete without eggs of some description. My fabric eggs can be used to decorate tables, hang on trees or are just great as presents for friends and family.

MAKES: 6 eggs

YOU WILL NEED:
- A4 sheet tracing paper
- Fabric pen
- Ruler
- Scissors (suitable for paper and fabric)
- Fabric (50cm x 50cm)
- Pins
- Sewing cotton
- Needle
- 50g polyester stuffing

TO CREATE THE TEMPLATE

1. Lay the tracing paper on the template provided (*bottom right, opposite*) and draw around it with a fabric pen. Cut the shape out. Place the fabric face down on a flat surface and place the template down on top, near an edge. Trace around it and move the template on, placing it as close as possible to the last panel and trace around it again. Repeat until you have 4 egg-shaped panels. Carefully cut out (*see image 1, right*).

TO SEW THE EGGS TOGETHER

2. Place 2 fabric egg panels face to face and pin in place. Sew one side together 5mm from the edge. Repeat with the other 2 fabric egg shapes (*see image 2, right*).

3. Sew the 2 halves together, pattern facing inwards (*see image 3*). Repeat this step with the other 2 panels.

4. Sew all 4 panels together (*see image 4, right*).

5. Leave 3cm open at the top of one seam so that the egg can be stuffed. When all 4 pieces have been sewn together, turn the fabric the right way out (*see image 5, right*).

6. Push the stuffing through the 3cm gap until the egg feels firm (*see image 6, right*). Use a small, neat hand stitch to close the opening of the egg. Repeat the above steps to create 5 more eggs. You will end up with an even half-dozen.

TIP Simply save an old egg carton and place the fabric eggs inside. Or attach a ribbon or piece of string to the top of the fabric eggs and hang from an Easter Tree made from cut branches (*see instructions for Valentine Tree, page 30*).

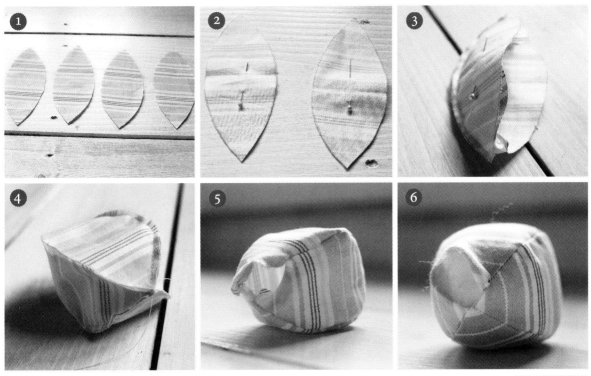

TEMPLATE FOR
EASTER EGG

*(also Fabric Pumpkin
Template, page 194)*

If you are preparing food for a picnic, apart from making sure that it tastes great, you also have to be pretty confident in its ability to travel well. You'll find that the recipes on the following pages will work if they are packed with care. Most can also be prepared the day before if wrapped and refrigerated. And why not take a flask of homemade punch or chilled lemonade with you (*see pages 184–85*). For me, this is all about priorities, meaning the more I do in advance, the more time I have to relax …

Oven-dried Tomato and Mozzarella Salad

SERVES: 4 (as a side);
2 (as a main)

INGREDIENTS
500g sweet cherry tomatoes
1 tbsp fresh oregano
3 tbsp extra virgin olive oil
200g mini mozzarella balls
2 medium garlic cloves,
    finely sliced
20 fresh basil leaves

Preheat the oven to 150°C/Gas 2. Wash the tomatoes and place them in a non-stick baking tin sprinkled with oregano. Drizzle with 1 tablespoon of olive oil.

Place in the preheated oven and roast the tomatoes for 1½ hours, until the skins have softened and are splitting. Remove the tomatoes from the oven and allow to cool in the tin.

Put the tomatoes in a medium-sized bowl and add in the mozzarella, garlic, basil leaves and the remaining olive oil.

Serving suggestion: The focaccia bread goes with this perfectly (*see pages 62–63*).

TIP Store in a bowl with a tight-fitting lid and keep in the fridge overnight. Also, by simply leaving out the mozzarella, this is a great dish for those vegan or lactose-intolerant friends.

A *Very* Tasty Asparagus Tart

MAKES: 6–8

INGREDIENTS
Unsalted butter, for greasing
500ml water
300g fine asparagus spears
1 round (225g) shortcrust
    pastry sheet
3 large eggs
1 large egg yolk
1 red onion, finely chopped
250ml double cream
100g Gruyère cheese,
    finely grated
60g Parmesan cheese, grated
Ground black pepper
Sea salt

SPECIAL EQUIPMENT
26cm-round flan/tart dish;
parchment paper; ceramic
baking beans, dried pulses or
uncooked rice

Preheat the oven to 180°C/Gas 4. Grease the flan dish with butter. In a large pan, over a medium heat, boil the water. Cook the asparagus for 1–2 minutes, or until it is just starting to soften. Drain and set to one side.

Place the pastry sheet in the greased flan dish, ensuring that the base and the sides are covered. Lay a sheet of parchment paper over the pastry and scatter the ceramic baking beans over the top. Bake for 10 minutes and remove from the oven. Remove the beans and parchment paper and leave to cool.

To make the filling, in a large bowl, use a large balloon whisk to beat the eggs and egg yolk together, getting as much air into the mixture as possible. Add the onion, cream, Gruyère cheese and 50g of the Parmesan. Whisk well and season with salt and pepper to taste.

Trim the ends of the asparagus spears to half the diameter of the pastry shell (about 13cm). Use the leftover asparagus trimmings to line the base of the pastry case. Cover with the egg and cheese mixture.

Put the tart on the middle shelf of the oven and bake for 15 minutes. Remove the tart from the oven and decorate the top with the remaining asparagus, laying the spear heads so that they fan out from the centre towards the pie crust.

Sprinkle the top of the tart with the remaining Parmesan cheese. Return to the top shelf of the oven and bake for a further 20–25 minutes until the top starts to turn a golden brown.

TIP Cover the tart securely with tin foil. Make sure it sits at the very top of your basket so it doesn't get spoilt on the journey. Don't forget a knife and napkins!

Variations

For Ricotta and Spinach Tart

Unsalted butter, for greasing; 1 round (225g) shortcrust pastry sheet; 400g fresh spinach; 1–2 tbsp water; 3 large eggs; 1 large egg yolk; 1 red onion, finely chopped; 250ml double cream; ½ tsp grated nutmeg; ground black pepper; sea salt; 100g ricotta cheese; 150g Stilton cheese; 50g walnuts, roughly chopped

Follow the oven and pastry instructions in the first two paragraphs on page 60.

Make the filling. In a saucepan with a lid, wilt the spinach along with the water over a low–medium heat for 3–4 minutes. Drain well, squeeze out any excess water and set to one side. Whisk the egg, onion and cream mixture for 2 minutes.

Whisk in the nutmeg and season to taste. Spoon the ricotta into the baked pastry case, making sure it evenly covers the base. Spread the wilted spinach out on top and pour the egg mixture over.

Sprinkle with crumbled Stilton and chopped walnuts. Bake for 30–35 minutes, or until the top starts to turn a golden brown.

Rosemary and Olive Focaccia Bread

MAKES: 8–10 slices

INGREDIENTS
500g strong white bread
    flour, plus extra
    for dusting
2 tsp salt
2 tsp sugar
10g fast-action dried yeast
300ml warm water
50g green olives, pitted
1 tbsp very finely chopped
    fresh rosemary
6 tbsp extra virgin olive oil

Dust a large non-stick roasting pan with flour.

Sift the flour into a large bowl and add the salt and sugar. Make a well in the middle of the mixture and pour in the yeast, adding the warm water to activate it.

Use your hands to bind the mixture into a loose dough. Then turn it out onto a clean, floured surface and knead for 4–5 minutes, until the dough doesn't stick to your hands. Mould it into a ball. If it is too sticky, just add a little more flour. If it is flakey, then add a dribble more water.

Return the dough to the bowl and cover with a clean, damp tea towel. Leave to prove in a warm place for about 40 minutes, or until the dough has doubled in size.

Remove the tea towel and use both hands to push the air out of the dough. Then roll it out to a thickness of about 2cm and to fit the length and width of the roasting pan.

Preheat oven to 230°C/Gas 8.

Press holes into the dough with the tips of your fingers at 4cm intervals. Fill with the olives and rosemary, then drizzle olive oil over the top. Leave to prove in a warm place for a further 40 minutes before placing it in the preheated oven.

Bake for 20 minutes, or until the bread has risen and is golden brown. If you tap the bottom of the bread, it should sound hollow.

Serving suggestion: Sprinkle with Maldon salt before serving.

 TIP Leave to cool and then wrap up tightly in tin foil. Take along a little bottle of extra virgin olive oil mixed with balsamic vinegar for dipping.

Spring Lemon Meringue Tartlets

These lemon meringue tartlets are very easy to make and are equally fit to serve at any party or as part of an afternoon tea.

MAKES: 4 individual tarts

INGREDIENTS

Pastry
50g unsalted cold butter, cut into cubes, plus extra for greasing
30g caster sugar
Good pinch salt
150g plain flour, plus a little extra for dusting
1 large egg

Lemon filling
50g caster sugar
2 large eggs
7 tsp cornflour
1 tsp vanilla extract
Zest and juice of 2 lemons

Meringue
2 large egg whites
100g caster sugar
½ tsp vanilla extract

SPECIAL EQUIPMENT
4 x 10cm loose-bottomed non-stick tartlet tins; parchment paper; ceramic baking beans, dried pulses or uncooked rice

Preheat the oven to 190°C/Gas 5. Grease the tartlet tins.

To make the pastry, in a large bowl add the butter, sugar, salt and sift in the flour. Use your fingertips to rub the ingredients together until the mixture has a crumb-like consistency. In a small bowl whisk the egg and add it to the pastry. Mix the ingredients together by hand until the dough is firm and can be shaped into a ball.

On a well-floured surface roll the pastry out to a thickness of about 5mm. Use an upturned bowl, slightly larger in circumference than the tartlet tin, and a sharp knife to cut out 4 circles of pastry.

Line the tins with the pastry circles, ensuring that the base and sides of the tins are lined evenly. Lay a sheet of parchment paper on top of each and add the baking weights. Cut off any excess pastry from around the rim. Transfer the pastry cases to a baking tray and bake for 7–8 minutes until half-baked. Take out of the oven and remove weights. Allow to cool.

To make the lemon filling, put the sugar, eggs, cornflour, vanilla extract and lemon zest and juice in a medium-sized bowl. Whisk until the mixture is smooth and glossy with no lumps. Divide the lemon filling evenly between the half-baked pastry shells.

Return the tartlets to the oven for a further 9–10 minutes or until the lemon filling has set (it should wobble slightly when very gently shaken back and forth).

To make the meringue, add the egg whites, sugar and vanilla extract to a clean bowl. Whisk for 4–5 minutes, or until the mixture forms soft peaks.

Using a tablespoon, generously spoon the meringue mix onto the top of the lemon tarts. Return them to the oven and bake for a further 15–20 minutes, or until the meringue turns a light golden brown colour and is slightly bouncy to touch and chewy to taste.

TIP This recipe can easily be adapted to create one impressive lemon meringue tart instead of individual ones. A lovely dessert for a Sunday lunch or dinner with friends.

Splendid Alliums …

Each year I grow alliums (also known as ornamental onions) in my garden. The variety I prefer is called Purple Sensation. It's fairly common, but I am really fond of the tall slender stalks and comical pom-pom heads of the flowers. I'd recommend planting each bulb 10cm deep in a sheltered but also sunny, well-drained spot during the autumn months.

Alliums are my flower of choice for the springtime Easter picnic as they make fabulous gifts for friends and are easy to transport in my bike basket or in the back of the car.

A few allium heads cut low down on the stem and tied loosely together with ribbon make a lovely gift. For the picnic though, just one cut allium head per guest is enough of a statement. They can then enjoy a single architectural flowerhead sitting majestically in a long glass stem vase or a recycled pretty glass bottle.

... and, of course, Rosemary

Although a pot of rosemary makes a lovely present, my garden isn't just a source for potential gifts for my loved ones. I often use rosemary throughout the year, as the recipe for rosemary and olive focaccia bread shows (*see pages 62–63*).

Rosemary is a very versatile herb and one associated with love, optimism and restful sleep. It is readily available in garden centres and supermarkets and is relatively cheap, as well. It's just such a great plant for home gardeners, as it's so easy to care for. It can last for up to 20 years, as long as it doesn't become waterlogged or too dry. If the soil looks thirsty, just water it.

I favour rosemary as it falls into what I call 'country kitchen instant additions' – things that are easy to grow, look pretty and are also functional. In this case, just by putting a few small terracotta or ceramic pots of fragrant rosemary on your window ledge, you not only have a great look, but, more importantly, you have a source of inspiration for those last-minute herbal additions to salads, condiments and dressings.

Robert's Birthday

OUR LOVED ONES' BIRTHDAYS SHOULD BE SPECIAL EVENTS in our year and since Robert is the most significant person in my life, this chapter is dedicated completely to him.

I met Robert in 2003, when I was living in London. My first thought when I laid eyes on him, was 'what a lovely face'. Of course, I was far too single, too carefree and too stupid to know that he would be very good for me. So, I had to wait another 18 months for us to get together. Once together, though, we were never to be parted, joined at the hip and unashamedly co-dependant. And, while life hasn't always been easy, we have each other and now the twins.

One day, when the twins were one year old and we had been married for just three years, Robert came home after a routine medical at work, carrying a bottle of champagne. He told me that he had leukaemia and that since we would get through it and be OK, we needed to celebrate. We sat on the swing seat in the garden and swigged the entire bottle between us. The next morning we woke up to begin a battle that would teach us a great deal about life, love and the universe.

There were times when I thought I would lose him, when he didn't respond to treatment, and the barrel I stared down during that time was long, dark and lonely. But he did make it through. In fact, he came home from hospital after six weeks of chemotherapy to find an entire photography crew in the garden doing the first shoot for this book and acted like it was nothing out of the ordinary. That's my husband. That is my Robert. And *that* is why he gets an entire chapter dedicated to his birthday.

Robert's birthday falls in the glorious month of April – and, as he prefers to keep things simple, the palette I have chosen for this occasion is white and green. The crafts are fairly restrained (for me), but are ones that I know he will appreciate. The table strips are placed along the length and width of the table, creating separate settings for each person. The felt flowers can be made in different shades of green and white and dotted around the table or placed together to make a single more impressive focal piece.

STEP *by* **STEP**

Decorative Table Strips

YOU WILL NEED:

- Fabric for 4 shorter strips (100cm x 50cm)
- Contrasting fabric for 2 longer strips (200cm x 25cm)
- Measuring tape
- Scissors (paper/fabric)
- Pins
- Sewing cotton
- Sewing machine
- Iron and ironing board

NOTE: These strips are for a table measuring 182 cm (l) x 88cm (w). Adjust the fabric lengths, as necessary, to fit your own table.

TO MAKE THE TABLE STRIPS

1. To make the shorter table strips, cut the fabric into 4 lengths, each measuring 92cm (l) x 12cm (w).

2. To make the longer table strips, cut the fabric into 2 lengths, each measuring 186cm (l) x 12cm (w).

3. Take 1 of the shorter table strips and fold it in half lengthways, patterned-side in. Pin together and sew 1cm from the edge. Do not sew the ends closed yet (*see image 1, right*).

4. Iron the hem out flat. Pin and then sew 1 end closed, 1.5cm from the edge (*see image 2, right*).

5. Cut any excess fabric from the corners for neatness. Turn the entire strip the right way out. Iron the strip again.

6. To close the other end of the strip, fold 2.5cm inside and then pin and sew 5mm from the edge (*see image 3, right*).

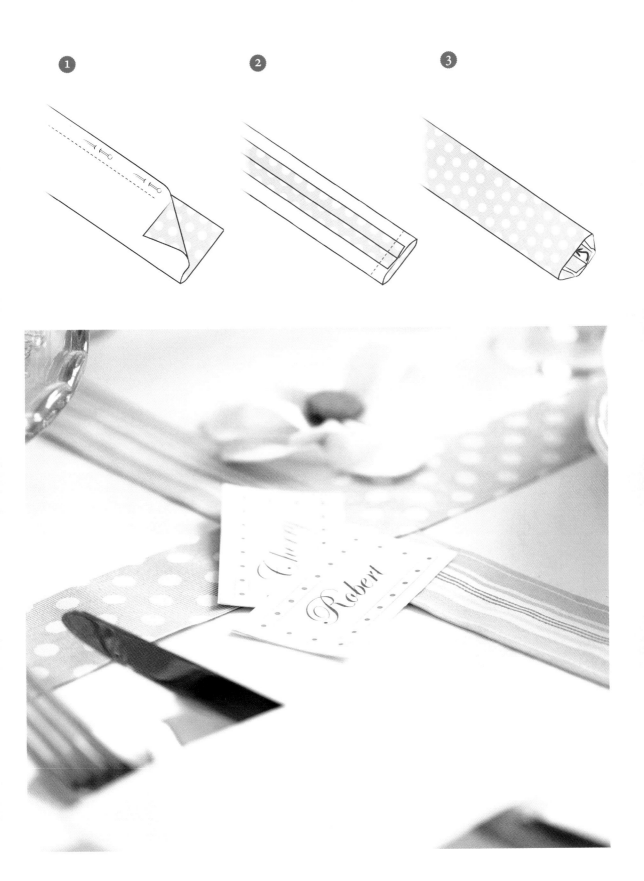

Decorative Felt Flower

 TO MAKE AND USE THE TEMPLATE

1. Lay the tracing paper over the templates (*top right*) and draw around them and cut out.

2. Using the templates cut 1 small circle, 6 large and 6 small petals from the green felt. Cut 1 large circle from the white felt.

 TO MAKE THE FLOWER AND CENTRE

3. To make the flower, start with the small petals. Pinch a fold into the centre of each petal and sew it together so that each felt petal is slightly gathered at the bottom tip (*see image 1, right*).

4. Take 3 of the small petals and sew them onto the small felt circle by their tips, spacing them out evenly around the circle (*see image 2, right*).

5. Sew the 3 remaining small petals onto the top of (and slightly overlapping with) the first 3 petals (*see image 3, right*).

6. Take the 6 large petals and join them by their tips with sewing cotton. Overlap the edges (*see image 4, right*).

7. Sew them to the underside of the small circle of flowers. Make sure that the stitching is on top of the flower centre as this will be covered (*see image 5, right*).

8. Place the 1 pence coin in the centre of the white felt circle (*see image 6, right*). Sew the sides together around the coin; the fabric should meet at the back of the coin. Place the white felt circle seam-side down in the middle of the felt flower and sew in place. Keep the stitches close to the flower centre.

MAKES: 1 flower

YOU WILL NEED:
- A4 sheet tracing paper
- Pencil
- Scissors (paper/fabric)
- Green felt
  (20cm x 20cm)
- White felt
  (20cm x 20cm)
- Sewing cotton
- Needle
- 1 pence coin

STAGE 1

TEMPLATE FOR FELT FLOWER

large petal   *small petal*   *large circle*   *small circle*

STAGE 2

TIP Attach to a hair band or large hair grip, or put a safety pin through the back of the flower for a charming brooch for your coat or jumper. Any of these things make lovely presents for your friends.

In this section, the menu also reflects the white-and-green theme of the meal. The pale white of the calamari rings is married with fresh wedges of lime; the green asparagus coupled with the creamy white–yellow of grated Parmesan cheese. The elderflower liqueur, used in the jellies, is a taste of spring, at a time when elderflower lines hedgerows everywhere. The clear jelly, with its mint leaf garnish and pale green frosting, is a light, refreshing finish to the meal.

Lime Calamari

SERVES: 6

INGREDIENTS
Calamari
100g self-raising flour, plus
extra for dusting
2 tbsp olive oil
½ tsp salt
2 tsp dried chilli flakes
150ml beer
    (I prefer Budweiser)
1 litre vegetable oil
500g calamari

Lime mayonnaise
1 large egg yolk
Zest and juice of 2 limes
1 tsp mustard powder
Salt
Ground white pepper
275ml sunflower oil

SPECIAL EQUIPMENT
Cooking thermometer;
slotted spoon

In a large mixing bowl, combine the flour, olive oil, salt and chilli flakes. Pour in the beer and mix until the batter is the consistency of double cream. Add more beer if it seems too thick. Leave the batter to chill for 15 minutes in the fridge.

Heat the vegetable oil in a large pan to 180°C; use the thermometer to test the temperature. You can double test the heat of the oil by dropping a teaspoon of batter into the pan. If it turns golden in colour after a few moments, it is ready.

Blot the calamari rings with kitchen roll to absorb any excess moisture. Lightly dust the rings in flour. Coat the calamari evenly in the batter mixture. Using a slotted spoon, lower the pieces into the oil, one at a time.

Fry for about 3 minutes or until golden, turning each piece once. Layer a plate with several sheets of kitchen roll and, using the spoon, remove the calamari from the oil and lay them on the plate for the paper to absorb any excess oil.

To make the mayonnaise, use a hand-held blender to mix together the egg yolk, 2 tablespoons of the lime juice and the mustard powder in a large jug. Season with salt and pepper and blend on a high speed until all the ingredients are fully combined.

On a slow speed, drizzle the oil into the jug. Mix until the liquid begins to emulsify and thicken. Once the mayonnaise has thickened to the point where it makes soft peaks, add the lime zest and rest of the lime juice to taste. Add more seasoning if necessary.

Serving suggestion: Take 2 rings and put 1 on top of the other on a Chinese ceramic spoon. Drop a teaspoon of mayonnaise on top and add some grated lime zest. Serve with a side plate of lime wedges.

TIP The mayonnaise will keep in the fridge for a few days and is great with chunky chips or with the fishcakes (*see pages 40–41*).

Robert's Pea and Prosciutto Spaghetti

Robert and I love Italy and have travelled there together several times. We love the food and this is my tribute to our times spent wandering the streets of Florence before finding a place for a romantic supper together.

SERVES: 4

INGREDIENTS
2 litres water
250g spaghetti
Olive oil, for frying
2 medium garlic cloves,
   finely chopped
250g fresh peas
100g prosciutto
½ tsp dried chilli flakes
10 fresh basil leaves
10g unsalted butter
Ground black pepper
30g Parmesan cheese, grated

In a large pan, over a high heat, salt the water and bring to the boil. Add the spaghetti and cook according to the packet instructions, until al dente. As the pasta softens, separate the strands with a fork.

In a non-stick frying pan, over a medium heat, gently heat the olive oil. Add the garlic and heat gently for 30 seconds, or until it starts to soften. Mix in the peas and stir for 2 minutes.

Cut 4 thin slices of prosciutto and put to one side. Chop the rest into small pieces and add to the frying pan, along with the chilli flakes. Sauté gently for 3 minutes before turning off the heat.

Drain the cooked pasta and pour it into a large warmed serving bowl. Rip up the basil leaves and add them and the butter to the bowl. Mix well.

Finally, fold in the pea and prosciutto mix and toss the pasta well.

Season with black pepper and a small sprinkle of Parmesan. Then, divide up equally between 4 warmed serving bowls.

Serving suggestion: Dry fry 4 whole pieces of prosciutto in a non-stick pan. Blot using kitchen paper to get rid of any excess oil. Put a piece on top of each bowl of pasta and garnish with basil leaves.

TIP This is suitable for a quick weekday supper. For a kids' teatime meal, simply serve without the whole prosciutto pieces and basil leaves.

Black Pepper Asparagus

SERVES: 4 (starter/side)

INGREDIENTS
1 litre water
400g fine green trimmed
    asparagus spears
Salt
50g unsalted butter
2 medium garlic cloves,
    finely chopped
50g Parmesan cheese, grated
2 tsp freshly ground black
    pepper

In a medium-sized pan, over a high heat, salt the water and bring to the boil. Trim the asparagus and place in the boiling water. Cook for 3–4 minutes. Turn the heat off and leave the asparagus in the water for the time being.

In a frying pan, over a medium heat, melt the butter. Stir in the garlic and heat gently for 30 seconds, or until it starts to soften. Take it off the heat and set to one side.

Drain the asparagus and divide the spears equally between the warmed serving plates. Drizzle with the melted garlic butter.

Mix the grated Parmesan and the ground black pepper with a spoon in a small bowl. Sprinkle it equally and evenly over the 4 portions of asparagus. Serve immediately.

Elderflower Jelly Shots

SERVES: 6

INGREDIENTS

Jelly
8 x fine leaf gelatine sheets
250ml water
250ml elderflower cordial
100ml elderflower liqueur

Frosting
1 large egg white
1 tbsp caster sugar
2 tsp mint green food
   colouring

SPECIAL EQUIPMENT
6 cylindrical shot glasses;
funnel

To make the jelly, in a large bowl soak the gelatine in cold water for 5 minutes. In a large pan, heat the water and elderflower cordial. Carefully remove the gelatine leaves from the bowl, and squeeze out any excess water. Add the softened gelatine to the pan and stir until it melts. Pour in the liqueur and stir well for 2 minutes. Take the pan off the heat and set aside to cool for 15 minutes.

To frost the glasses, in a clean bowl lightly whisk the egg white for 60–90 seconds, until it foams. Add the caster sugar and mint food colouring and whisk until combined.

Take the shot glasses and dip the rim of each glass into the frosting. Place in the fridge; leave for 15 minutes to allow the frosting to harden. Use the funnel to pour the jelly into the individual shot glasses. Put the jellies on a tray and refrigerate for 4–5 hours, or overnight.

Serving suggestion: Place shot glasses on a plate with a teaspoon and a fresh sprig of mint.

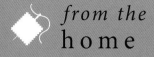

Setting Robert's Table

My aim is to create a clean and fresh look for Robert's table, perfect for a springtime supper. It's both simple and elegant, without being cluttered. Here are a few tips on how to achieve this effect so you can try it too:

- ### THE TABLE SETTINGS

  Cover the table with a freshly washed and pressed white cotton tablecloth. Lay 2 long green table strips parallel to each other, lengthways down the middle of the table. Lay the 4 shorter green table strips across the 2 runners at equal intervals. This splits the table into 6 sections that can be dressed, decorated or divided up as you wish. Place 8 felt flowers around the table, 2 per setting.

- ### MENU WRAPS

  Make menu wraps to tuck around the cutlery. To do this, use a computer to create a green-and-white border template for an A5 sheet. Type out the menu (use Century font; point size 13) and make sure the text is centred, allowing a margin of 4cm on each side. Print and trim the paper to measure 9cm (h) x 21cm (w). Fold each side back by 4cm; this allows the centred text to be readable. Wrap the paper around the cutlery and lay flat on a side plate. The weight of the cutlery resting on the paper will keep the wrap in place.

- ### TABLE DECORATION

  Repot 2 fresh green basil plants into simple white plant pots and place on the table. As well as visually pleasing, this also allows guests to tear off basil leaves if they want to add them to their food. Teamed with white crockery and lots of glass – water jugs, water and wine glasses and candlesticks and votive holders for when it gets darker – when the candles are lit, the table is simply but elegantly dressed.

Afternoon Tea

I HAVE BEEN LUCKY ENOUGH to 'take tea' in some of the most beautiful places in the world, and I have a great affection for a ritual that is fairly far removed from my everyday life. Some of the most important events in my family's lives have happened while enjoying afternoon tea. My sister received a surprise marriage proposal, in front of our whole family, during tea at the Ritz, and I celebrated my own engagement in the tearooms at the very same hotel.

I love hosting Afternoon Tea in my own home and there are several reasons why it is one of my favourite things to do, particularly in the month of June. It's an occasion when the girls and I have a lovely excuse to get dressed up during the day and become too excited over very small sandwiches, and it's also a great excuse for me to explore new and more complicated ways of baking cakes with fancy French names. And, finally, it makes complete sense for me to have a sideboard and a standard lamp on the lawn – but more on that later in this chapter.

The thing that really makes hosting Afternoon Tea worthwhile is that – when it's over – everyone looks happy, contented, calm and peaceful, and many murmur, 'that was lovely; really lovely'. Personally, I don't think you can ever have too much loveliness.

In this chapter I want to take you through hosting a simple Afternoon Tea, complete with sandwiches (crusts cut off), traditional cakes and those French ones I mentioned earlier. I have also included a couple of crafts that you'll decorate your table with forever, certainly not just for Afternoon Teas.

The following crafts are about making your table the centrepiece for Afternoon Tea. The boxed tablecloth and chair slipcovers are relatively easy to make and transform my boring oblong table and chairs into something much more clean and fresh.

STEP by STEP Chair Slipcover

YOU WILL NEED:

- A chair
- Fabric (3m; I use a 50/50 cotton/linen mix)
- Scissors
- Measuring tape
- Cutting mat
- Pencil
- Pins
- Sewing cotton
- Sewing machine
- Iron and ironing board

MY CHAIR MEASUREMENTS:

- Chair height:
  97cm *(total height)*
- Back:
  38cm *(width)*
  53cm *(height from seat up)*
- Seat:
  43cm *(front width)*
  39cm *(back width)*
  36cm *(depth)*
  45cm *(height from floor)*

TO CREATE THE FABRIC PIECES

Start by cutting out the following:

Seat Back Panel: 65cm x 55cm
Back Panel: 105cm x 50cm
Seat Panel: 50cm x 45cm
Side Panels x 2:   50cm x 50cm each
Front Panel x 1:   50cm x 50cm

TO MAKE THE FRONT AND BACK OF THE SLIPCOVER

1. On a flat surface, place the 55cm edge of the seat back panel fabric face down in the centre and on top of the 50cm edge of the back panel. Pin in place 3cm down from the top edge and sew together. Place the fabric over the top of the chair. Carefully line up the sewn seam with the top back edge of the chair. Refer to image 1, right, for the positioning. Pin one of the open sides closed.

2. On the unpinned side, fold the seat back panel fabric around the chair and under the back panel. Tuck the seat back panel back under itself so that the fabric lines up with the edge of the chair.

3. When tucked into place, pull taut and pin at the back all the way down to where the chair's seat is attached to the back frame. Repeat this process for the other side of the chair.

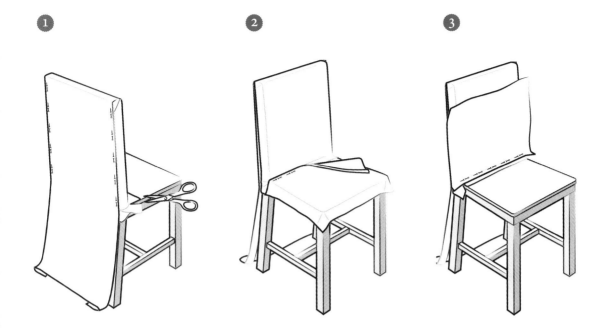

4. Turn the fabric inside out (with the pins still in place on the outside to hold it together). Follow the seams and re-pin the fabric where the existing pins are. Remove the existing pins as you go.

5. Turn the slipcover the right way out and place it over the top of the chair to make sure that it fits snugly. Make any necessary adjustments and remove it again. Turn it inside out and sew the seams closed.

6. Once the 2 chair back panels have been sewn together, turn the fabric the right way out, place over the chair and make a slit of 5–6cm on either side of the fabric, at the point where it meets the back bottom edge of the chair seat (*see image 1*).

TO MAKE AND ATTACH THE SLIPCOVER SEAT

7. Place the seat panel fabric onto the seat of the chair; the 50cm edge should run along the back. Position the fabric in the middle of the seat so that the fabric sits 4–5cm over on all 4 sides (*see image 2*); this is for hemming. Fold a 3cm hem under along the back edge of the seat panel. Pin to the seat back panel.

8. Remove the cover, turn inside out and re-pin the same seam on the inside of the fabric, removing the outside pins as you go (*see image 3*). Place the cover, inside out, onto the chair (the seam should sit parallel to the back of the seat). Sew together, turn the right way out and place back over the chair.

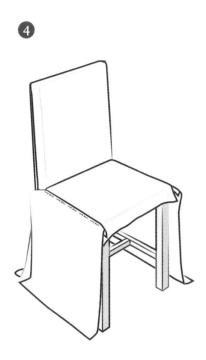

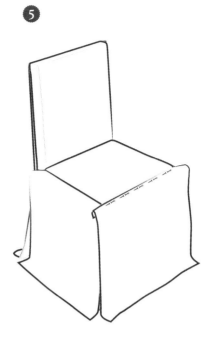

TO ATTACH THE 2 SIDE PANELS AND THE FRONT PANEL

9. Allowing for a 2.5cm hem, pin the top edges of the 2 side panels to either side of the seat panel, leaving 2.5cm of unpinned fabric also at the bottom edges (*see image 4*).

10. Re-pin the underside while still in place on the chair. Stay as close to the original pin line as possible. Remove the cover and sew together, removing all pins as you go. Place back on the chair.

11. Pin the remaining front panel to the front edge of the seat panel (*see image 5*); allow a hem of 2.5cm. Re-pin the underside, staying as close to original pin line as possible. Remove slipcover and sew together, removing the pins as you do so.

TO FINISH OFF

12. Place the slipcover onto the chair, right way out. Tuck the side panel hems behind the edges of the back panel fabric (*see image 6, right*). Fold the back panel fabric (remaining on either side) under into a double hem; the outer seam should be in line with the seat back's seam. Pin the fabrics in place and then sew together. Repeat this step to create the two front side panels of the chair cover (*see image 7, right*).

13. Finish by double hemming and pinning (around 2cm per hem) all of the raw edges of the seat cover. The hems should sit just above the ground. Remove the seat cover to sew all of the hems in place. Iron and place the completed slipcover over the top of the chair (*see photo, right*).

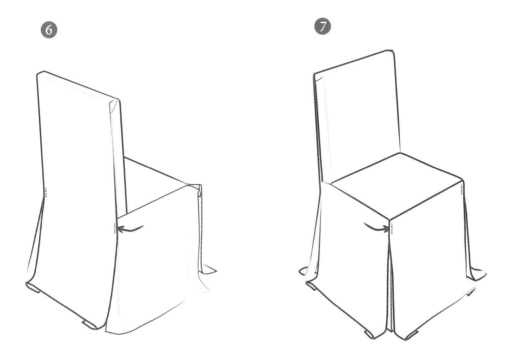

A Boxed Tablecloth

1. Lay the fabric over the table. Measure the fabric to fit the table top and add a drop of about 25cm (including the hem) all the way around. Cut out fabric (*see image 1*).

2. Lay the fabric out on the floor. Create a double hem (1cm per hem) all the way around. Pin and sew in place (*see image 2, right*).

TO CREATE A BOXED CORNER

3. Place the fabric face down on the table and drape it so that it has a 23cm even drop. Starting with the far left corner measure 23cm along from the corner on both sides and pin at these points. Fold the corner in so that the 2 pins meet. Use additional pins to secure from the bottom edge upwards in a straight line to the corner of the table (*see image 3, right*). Sew from the bottom hem of the tablecloth to the top of the row of pins. Repeat this step with each of the remaining 3 corners.

TO FINISH THE TABLECLOTH

4. Once all the corners are sewn and 'boxed' cut the excess corner fabric off 2cm from the hemmed edge (*see image 4, right*). Iron the hems flat on the inside of the tablecloth. Turn the right way out and place on your table (*see photo, right*).

YOU WILL NEED:
- Fabric of your choice (250cm (l) x 150cm (w); I used a 50/50 cotton/linen mix)
- Measuring tape
- Pins
- Scissors
- Sewing cotton
- Sewing machine
- Iron and ironing board

NOTE: This tablecloth was made to fit a table measuring 182cm x 88cm, but adjust your measurements to fit your own table.

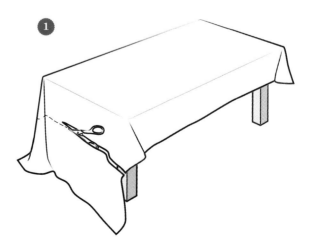

I don't like rules and rail against them 99 per cent of the time. So I'm not going to give you a list to follow for the menu, but just let you have some of my favourite recipes. I am going to add, though, that if you need to use shop-bought bread, pastry or jam, that's fine. This is about spending time with the people you care about and having a great time, not hours spent slaving away in the kitchen.

Afternoon Egg and Cress Sandwiches

MAKES: 8 finger
sandwiches, 2 tiers high

INGREDIENTS
2 litres water
6 large hard-boiled eggs
2 tbsp mayonnaise
2 x 20g packets cress, cut
Salt
Ground black pepper
Unsalted butter, room
    temperature for spreading
6 slices good-quality
    white bread

*NOTE: See page 41 for a
recipe and method for making
mustard mayonnaise. Simply
leave out the Dijon mustard
and mustard powder to
create a basic mayonnaise.*

In a large saucepan, bring the water to simmering point. Place the eggs in the water and leave to cook for 6–7 minutes (6 minutes leaves the centres slightly squidgy inside).

Remove the eggs from the water and place them in a bowl of cold water. Once cool, remove the shells and put the eggs in a large mixing bowl.

Add the mayonnaise, the cut cress and seasoning. Use a fork to mash together until the ingredients are completely blended.

To make the sandwiches, spread a thin layer of butter onto one side of each slice of bread.

Place a heaped spoonful of the egg mixture onto 4 slices of bread; use a knife to spread the mixture out evenly.

To create a sandwich, take 1 slice of egg-covered bread and lay it on top of another. Lay one of the buttered slices of bread face down on top. Press down lightly with the palm of your hands to hold the ingredients in place. Carefully cut the crusts off with a sharp knife before slicing the sandwich into 4 even-sized fingers.

Repeat to create the second round of sandwiches and arrange on a cake stand or serving plate.

Variations

For Chicken and Pea Shoot Sandwiches

1kg whole chicken; 2 tbsp aioli mayonnaise; 6 slices good-quality white bread; unsalted butter, room temperature; 40g pea shoots; salt; ground black pepper

Immerse the chicken in a large pan of boiling water. Cover and simmer for 45 minutes, or until cooked. Remove the chicken from the water and allow to cool then carve the meat. In a large bowl use 2 forks to shred the meat before mixing in the aioli mayonnaise and seasoning. Make the sandwiches *(see page 94)*, but use the chicken mayonnaise mix and pea shoots instead of the egg and cress.

For Smoked Salmon, Cream Cheese and Dill sandwiches

200g cream cheese; 20g fresh dill, finely chopped; 6 slices good-quality brown bread; unsalted butter, room temperature; 200g smoked salmon; ground black pepper

In a medium-sized bowl, mix the dill, cream cheese and seasoning. Create the sandwiches as before, but replace the egg mix with a layer of cream cheese and a slice of smoked salmon.

Lemon and Poppy Seed Muffins

MAKES: 10

INGREDIENTS
Muffins
230g caster sugar
200g unsalted butter,
    softened
4 large eggs
½ tsp vanilla extract
320g self-raising flour
100ml freshly squeezed
    lemon juice (2 lemons)
3 tsp grated lemon zest
2 tsp poppy seeds

Icing
200g icing sugar
2–3 tbsp water
2–3 tsp poppy seeds

SPECIAL EQUIPMENT
silicone muffin tray

Preheat the oven to 190°C/Gas 5. Cream the sugar and butter in the bowl of a free-standing mixer with a paddle attachment, until light and fluffy.

Separate the eggs. Add the yolks and vanilla to the bowl and mix together.

In a clean bowl, use a whisk attachment to beat the egg whites until they start to stiffen slightly; then add them to the bowl. Sift in the flour and add the lemon juice, lemon zest and poppy seeds. Use the paddle attachment to mix the ingredients together until combined and the batter is smooth and creamy.

Spoon the batter into the holes of the silicone muffin tray, until about ¾ full. Place in the preheated oven and bake for 25 minutes, or until golden brown on top. Allow the muffins to cool in the muffin tray before removing them (or they will stick).

To make the icing, mix the water and icing sugar together until smooth and slightly runny (add more water if necessary). Drizzle the icing over the top of the muffins. Finish with a sprinkle of poppy seeds.

A *Very* Easy Muffin Case

YOU WILL NEED:

- A4 sheet tracing paper
- Pen/pencil
- Card/piece of wallpaper
- Scissors

Use the tracing paper to carefully draw around the muffin template and cut out.

Place on the back of the card or wallpaper and draw around. Cut out the template, remembering to include the incision line.

Construct the muffin case by placing the tab through the cut.

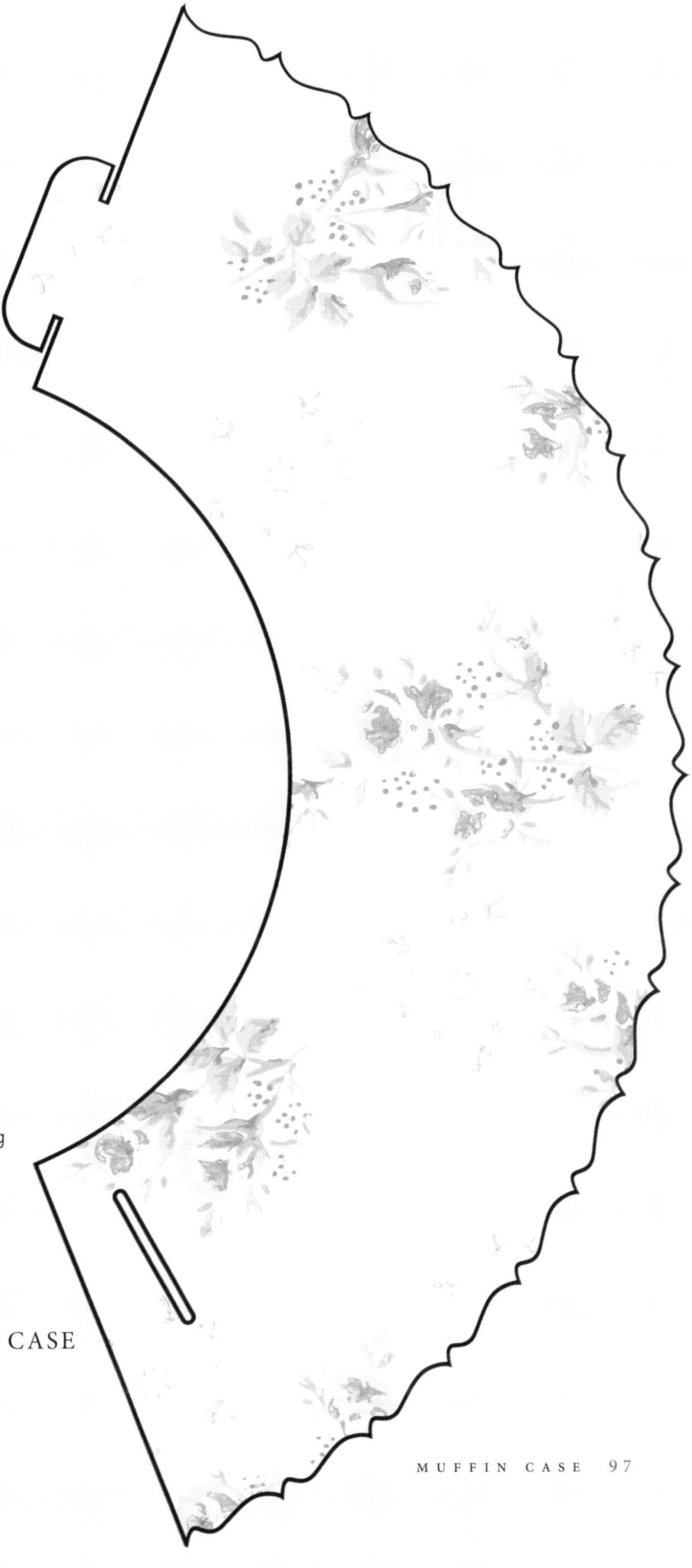

TEMPLATE FOR MUFFIN CASE

scale 90%

Mille-feuille

MAKES: 6

INGREDIENTS
500g puff pastry
350g fresh raspberries
Icing sugar, for dusting

Crème Pâtissière
400ml full fat milk
160ml double cream
2 vanilla pods
4 large egg yolks
160g granulated sugar
4 heaped tbsp cornflour

SPECIAL EQUIPMENT
Parchment paper; Tongs;
piping bag with a medium-
sized nozzle

Preheat the oven to 190°C/Gas 5. Line a baking tray with parchment paper.

TO MAKE THE PASTRY SLICES

Roll the pastry out flat until it is about 3–4mm thick. Cut 18 oblong-shaped pieces, each measuring 12cm x 5cm. Place on a baking tray and bake (in batches, if necessary) for 10 minutes. Remove from the oven and allow to cool on a wire rack.

TO MAKE THE CRÈME PÂTISSIÈRE

Pour the milk and double cream into a large pan. Use a sharp knife to split the vanilla pods all the way down the middle and open them out fully with your fingertips. Put the pods in the pan.

Over a low heat, bring the cream and milk slowly to the boil. Remove from the heat and cover the pan with a lid. Allow it to stand for about 10 minutes to enable the vanilla to infuse the milk and cream. Then, remove the vanilla pods with the tongs and discard.

In a large, clean bowl, use a balloon whisk to beat together the egg yolks and the sugar. Add the cornflour and whisk again. Mix the egg liquid into the warm milk and return the pan to a low heat. Lightly beat the mixture until it starts to thicken, then immediately remove the pan from the heat.

Transfer the crème pâtissière to a separate bowl. Cover with cling film and refrigerate for at least 1 hour. When the mixture has chilled, spoon the crème pâtissière into the piping bag with a nozzle.

TO CREATE THE MILLE-FEUILLE

Take 3 pieces of the oblong-shaped baked pastry and lay them flat on a plate. Evenly pipe 4 pastry cream balls onto each side of the first pastry piece. Place a raspberry on top of each cream ball. Then do the same with the second pastry strip. Place it on top of the first piece. Seal the two layers with the third piece of pastry.

Repeat the above stage 5 more times and then dust the 6 mille-feuille with icing sugar before serving.

Rose Cream Shortbread

MAKES: 6

INGREDIENTS
Shortbread
250g unsalted butter,
    softened
100g caster sugar
250g plain flour, plus a
    little extra for dusting
Granulated sugar,
    for sprinkling

Rose cream filling
50g unsalted butter,
    softened
400g icing sugar, sifted
2–3 tbsp water
1 tsp Le Syrup de Monin
    Rose
2–3 drops rose food
    colouring

SPECIAL EQUIPMENT
Baking tray (20cm x 30cm);
parchment paper; 6cm
circular cookie cutter; piping
bag with a medium-sized
nozzle

Preheat the oven to 180°C/Gas 4. Line the baking tray with the parchment paper.

In the bowl of a free-standing mixer with a paddle attachment, beat the butter and the caster sugar together, until smooth.

Sift in the flour and continue mixing until a soft dough has formed. Remove the dough from the bowl and mould into a loose ball.

On a clean surface, flatten the dough into a thick disc shape. Wrap the dough in cling film and chill for 30 minutes.

Remove the dough from the fridge and on a well-floured surface, roll the dough out until it is 1cm thick and to roughly the size of the baking tray.

Place the dough in the tray and use a fork to prick holes as evenly as possible in the surface. Sprinkle generously with granulated sugar. Bake the dough for about 20 minutes, or until it is golden on top.

Remove from oven. Use the cookie cutter to cut out the shortbread rounds while still warm, making sure that there is as little wastage as possible. Leave to cool before filling.

To make the icing, blend the butter, icing sugar and water together in the bowl of a free-standing mixer. Add the rose syrup and colouring, mixing until it forms a smooth paste.

Transfer the rose cream to the piping bag. Place 3 rounds of shortbread on a plate and pipe the filling on top. Then, finish by topping each with the remaining shortbread.

TIP This can be used a gift for loved ones, friends, or as a parting gift from Afternoon Tea.

Lovely Fruit Slices

MAKES: 14–16

INGREDIENTS
200g demerara sugar
200g unsalted butter, softened
1 tsp ground cinnamon
1 tsp mixed spice
Salt
4 large eggs
5 tbsp full-fat milk
Zest and juice of 1 orange
Zest and juice of 1 lemon
700g mixed fruit (sultanas,
    currants, candied peel)

SPECIAL EQUIPMENT
2lb loaf tin; parchment
paper

Preheat the oven to 190°C/Gas 5. Grease the loaf tin and line with the parchment paper.

In the bowl of a free-standing mixer, with a paddle attachment, beat the sugar and butter together until light and fluffy. Sift in the flour, cinnamon, mixed spice and salt and mix well. Then, mix in the eggs and blend until creamy. Slowly pour in the milk, blending as you do so. Stir in the citrus zest, juice and dried fruit, mixing well until fully combined.

Pour the cake batter into the tin and use a spatula to evenly distribute the mixture. Bake in the oven for 40–45 minutes, or until golden brown on top and a knife inserted into the cake comes out clean.

Allow the cake to cool completely before removing it from the tin and cut into even slices.

ERRATUM

The recipe on page 102 for *Lovely Fruit Slices* should read as shown below.

Lovely Fruit Slices

MAKES: 14–16

INGREDIENTS
200g demerara sugar
200g unsalted butter, softened
300g plain flour
1 tsp ground cinnamon
1 tsp mixed spice
Salt
4 large eggs
5 tbsp full-fat milk
Zest and juice of 1 orange
Zest and juice of 1 lemon
700g mixed fruit (sultanas,
    currants, candied peel)

SPECIAL EQUIPMENT
2lb loaf tin; parchment
paper

Preheat the oven to 190°C/Gas 5. Grease the loaf tin and line with the parchment paper.

In the bowl of a free-standing mixer, with a paddle attachment, beat the sugar and butter together until light and fluffy. Sift in the flour, cinnamon, mixed spice and salt and mix well. Then, mix in the eggs and blend until creamy. Slowly pour in the milk, blending as you do so. Stir in the citrus zest, juice and dried fruit, mixing well until fully combined.

Pour the cake batter into the tin and use a spatula to evenly distribute the mixture. Bake in the oven for 40–45 minutes, or until golden brown on top and a knife inserted into the cake comes out clean.

Allow the cake to cool completely before removing it from the tin and cut into even slices.

... *and* a Cup of Tea

There is nothing more comforting than a properly brewed cup of tea and yet the method of making tea is much debated. Do you put milk in before or after? How long should you leave it to brew? Anyway, here are a few tips:

- Use a good quality loose-leaf tea or tea bag (stored in an air-tight container at room temperature).
- Use fresh (pre-) boiling water.
- Make sure you put the right amount in – use 1 tea bag or 1 teaspoon of loose-leaf tea for each cup.
- Allow the tea to brew for the recommended time before pouring it (*see below*).
- Milk in after the tea is how I take mine.

- ### TYPE OF TEA
  It's pretty safe to say, the better the quality of tea, the better the cup of tea. Quality teas can be steeped up to 3 times.

- ### HOW MUCH
  1 rounded teaspoon of leaf tea or a teabag and cup of water per person is a good rule of thumb.

- ### WATER
  The more oxygenated the water, the better it is for the tea. Don't use reboiled water for this reason.

- ### TEMPERATURE
  For good leaf tea, the tea should be below boiling (ideally white teas are best made with water at about 70°C; green and black teas at around 85°C). So, ideally turn off the kettle just before it boils. Tea made with water at 100°C will be far less tasty because the amino acids that produce the tea's flavour dissolve at lower temperatures than tannin.

A Room Outdoors

There's nothing more lovely than having tea outside and I have used this occasion to create another one of my favourite scenes; a beautiful room outdoors.

The room I've created in my garden resembles an old-fashioned dining room, like the one my nana had in her house, with a tea trolley, sideboard and family photographs everywhere. At the heart of it lies my table, newly dressed with a crisp white boxed tablecloth, and this is where we lay out the food and drink to take tea.

To create this setting, I've taken a few of my favourite pictures from my living room and hung them, rather haphazardly it has to be said, on the garden hedgerow. Jodie and I carry out armchairs to sit on, a sideboard and even a standard lamp (for which you, of course, need an outside socket or an extension lead).

I set the table with cutlery, plates and napkins and then the piles of sandwiches and cakes on pretty plates and cake stands come out, along with the lemon and poppy seed muffins in their homemade cases.

The subtle perfume of roses fills the air from the 15 or so pink, lilac and cream rose bushes, planted out over the past 5 years. I've used a few blooming heads to decorate the table.

A Children's Party

I'M NOT GOING TO LIE TO YOU, I think that throwing a birthday party for your own child or children is a real challenge. It takes planning, coordination, forethought, help and the patience of a saint. I can honestly say that it is easier to throw parties for children when you are not one of the parents than when you are. Which is why I want to start this chapter by reassuring you that small children are just as happy running around the garden with sticky hands and sticky faces, with other sticky children, as they are watching Cirque du Soleil, whom you've mortgaged your house to hire for the day!

There's one thing that often gets forgotten when you are the parent hosting the party for your child or children; occasionally you'd like to be able to stop, sit down for just a second, and watch the children having a great time. But all too often you end up in the kitchen, or with your head stuck in a cupboard searching out some extra straws, and miss the priceless look on your son or daughter's face when something wonderful happens.

In this chapter, I have included quite a few crafts for you to choose from and some recipes that are easy to make and sit well in the 'sort of healthy junk food' category. Please don't run yourself ragged attempting to make and cook everything for one party. Think about what your children would love, please ask for some help from other parents both before and during the event and remember that the only thing, the ONLY thing, your children and their friends will remember is the fun they had on the day. And that includes you being able to have fun with them.

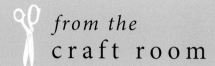

A World of Magic

This chapter is all about creating a special world for children – one of colour and fun, but one that's also safe and practical. All of the following crafts can be used time and time again. The giant toadstools, which follow, are multi-functional and can be used in the garden, but also look great in a child's bedroom. The wigwam is based on one that I made for my nieces, which gave them hours of fun. And the initialled party bags are just an extra touch and are helpful as you'll know exactly who gets what at the end of the party.

STEP by STEP

A Giant Toadstool

The following pages (*pages 111–15*) give instructions on how to assemble this giant toadstool in 3 easy stages:

 STAGE 1 shows you how to make the base.

 STAGE 2 provides the template for making the toadstool head.

 STAGE 3 shows you how to decorate and finish the toadstool.

YOU WILL NEED:

Base
- A1 piece white card (300gsm)
- Measuring tape
- Sticky tape
- Scissors (paper/fabric)
- White felt (1m x 1m)
- 1 skein red embroidery thread
- Embroidery needle
- Craft glue

Head
- A1 piece red card (300gsm)
- Tracing paper roll (841mm x 20m)
- Pencil and compass
- Red felt (1.5m x 1m)
- 2 skeins white embroidery thread
- 500g polyester stuffing

Decoration
- Leftover white felt
- Green felt (50cm x 25cm)

 TO MAKE THE 50CM-HIGH BASE

1. Take the card and roll it at an angle to create a cone with a bottom diameter of 17cm and top diameter of 11cm. Tape the base along the seam and trim the top and bottom edges so that the cone is level. The test is if the base can stand up when set on the ground (*see image 1*).

2. Cover the base in white felt and sew into place, trimming off any excess felt. Set this aside to use for the toadstool spots in Stage 3. Use the red embroidery thread to sew along the vertical seam, where the felt meets. There will be excess felt at either end of the base. Trim some off to use for the spots, as above, but leave enough to tuck inside the cone, gluing the felt down inside (*see image 2*).

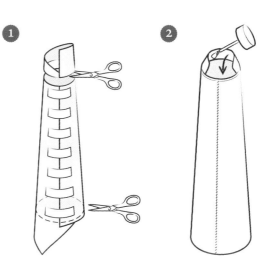

46cm diameter

TEMPLATE FOR TOADSTOOL WITH TABS
scale 50%

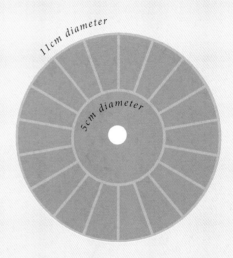

11cm diameter

5cm diameter

TO CREATE THE TOADSTOOL HEAD

1. Take a piece of tracing paper and draw over the template (*left*). On the red card, first trace the outer circle (diameter 46cm) and cut it out. Use a pencil to clearly mark the centre of the circle (*see white spot, left*). Then draw the second circle (diameter 11cm) and finally the third circle (diameter 5cm).

2. Use sharp scissors to make a small incision in the centre of the smallest circle. From this point start cutting the centre of this circle out. Remove it and then make the tabs by cutting 18 slits at equal intervals all the way around the edge of the smallest circle up to the line of the second circle (*see image 3*). Fold these tabs over; they will be glued to the base. Set the card aside.

3. Take the red felt and use a pencil and compass to draw and cut out a circle (diameter 49cm). Mark the centre of the felt circle and, using the compass, draw a circle 11cm in diameter. Cut this circle out from the centre of the felt. Place the circular card template onto the felt circle, so that it is centered and cut out the centre. The extra material around the edges provides a hem allowance of 1.5cm all around.

4. Push the toadstool base through the 11cm-diameter red felt circle. Use white embroidery thread to handstitch the piece of red felt to the white felt covering the top of the base base (*see image 4*).

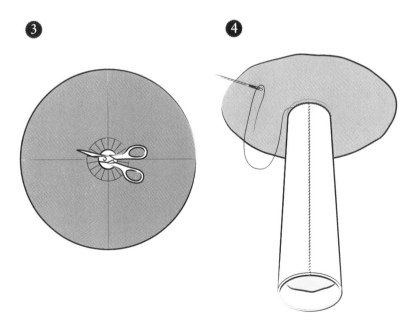

5. Place the red card with the tabs on top of the red felt now attached to the toadstool base. Glue the tabs onto the inside of the base (*see image 5*). Cut out a felt circle with a 70cm diameter from the remaining red felt. Pin this circle to the piece of red felt attached to the toadstool base, making sure that the tabbed piece of card is sandwiched between them. As the top piece is much bigger than the bottom, it will need pleats (*see image 6*). Fold the fabric at 25cm intervals and pin into place.

6. Use white embroidery thread to sew the edges of the two top pieces of the toadstool together, leaving a 10cm gap open through which to stuff the top (*see image 6*). Push the filling inside, making sure it fills out the top properly, then sew the gap closed.

STAGE 1 — TO DECORATE THE TOADSTOOL

7. Use the pencil and compass to draw and cut out 10 circles (8cm diameter) from the leftover white felt. Position them evenly over the top of the toadstool (*see photo, opposite*) and glue them down with craft glue.

8. On the piece of green felt, use a pencil to draw grass (no higher than 20cm and to a width of between 3cm and 5cm). Cut this out, making sure that the bottom edge is even. Line the straight edge up with the bottom of the toadstool base and glue the felt grass in place (*see image 7*).

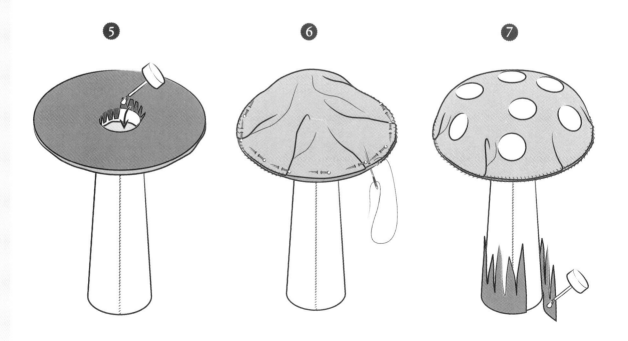

Children's Wigwam

YOU WILL NEED:

- 3 x 1m wooden poles
- 100ml tester pot paint
- Paintbrush
- 2m string
- Top panel fabric (3m (l) x 22cm (w))
- Wigwam fabric (3m (l) x 1.14m (w))
- Pins
- Sewing cotton
- Sewing machine
- 8m giant ric-rac
- Scissors
- Measuring tape
- 1.5m cord
- 5 metal tent pegs

TO CREATE THE FRAME

1. Paint the wooden poles; leave to dry. Tie the 3 poles together at the top using the string (*see image 1*). Loop the string under and around the poles, then secure in a knot. Once the string is secure, push the poles out at a 45° angle, creating a triangle shape with them. If the string is tied tightly enough the poles will stand up by themselves.

TO MAKE THE WIGWAM

2. Fold and pin a double hem (1cm per hem) along the shorter edges of the top panel fabric. Sew in place. Along the longer edges of the top panel fabric, fold in 1cm from the edge, pin in place and then fold the whole fabric in half (*see image 2*). Pin the long open edges together.

3. Sew the 3m sides together leaving the short ends open as this will be the channel for the cord to go through. Take the wigwam fabric and create a double hem (1cm per hem), along the 2 sides and bottom edge. Do not hem the top. Pin and sew a double hem (*see image 3*).

4. Pin the top panel fabric to the unhemmed top of the wigwam fabric, pattern-side up (*see image 4, left*). Ensure the folded edge of the top panel fabric is attached and not the sewn edge. Sew in place 5mm from the edge.

TO MAKE THE TIES AND LOOPS

5. Pin the ric-rac along the outside hemmed edges and bottom of the wigwam fabric. Sew down the centre of the ric-rac to secure in place (*see image 5*).

6. To make the tent peg loops, cut 5 lengths of ric-rac, each 16cm long. Pin in place along the bottom of the wigwam (50cm apart from one another). Sew in place (*see image 6*).

7. To make the door ties, cut 4 x 37cm lengths of ric-rac. Lay the wigwam fabric out on the floor. Measure 50cm in from both side edges and measure up from the bottom edge by 50cm. Where the 2 points meet, pin the end of a piece of ric-rac to each point. Turn the fabric over and repeat on the other side so that 2 pieces of ric-rac are face to face. Sew in place.

TO SET UP THE WIGWAM

8. Thread the cord all the way through the channel at the top the wigwam. Pull the fabric tight along the cord to create gathers. Secure the ends of the cord to the top of the wigwam poles in a knot or bow. Spread out the the 3 pole legs equally on even ground and arrange the wigwam cover around it. Secure in place by hammering the tent pegs through the loops into the ground (*see photo, above*).

Personalised Felt Party Bag

STEP *by* STEP

MAKES: 1 bag: 11.5cm (h) x 15cm (w) x 11 (d)

YOU WILL NEED:

Bag

- 2 x contrasting coloured felt (31cm x 23cm)
- Measuring tape
- Scissors
- 1 skein embroidery thread in a complementary colour
- Embroidery needle

Decoration

- A4 sheet paper
- Pencil
- Scissors (paper/fabric)
- Leftover end fabric
- Pins

TO CREATE THE PANELS/HANDLE

1. To create the front, back and base of the bag fold 1 sheet of felt in half and cut. Fold and cut those 2 sections in half to create 4 pieces measuring 15.5cm x 11.5cm (*see image 1, right*). Put the leftover fabric to one side.

2. To create the end panels, take the contrasting coloured sheet of felt and cut out 2 pieces measuring 11.5cm x 11.5cm (*see image 2, right*).

3. Using the leftover end panel fabric, cut out a piece measuring 20cm x 6cm. This will become the bag's handle. Set it to one side.

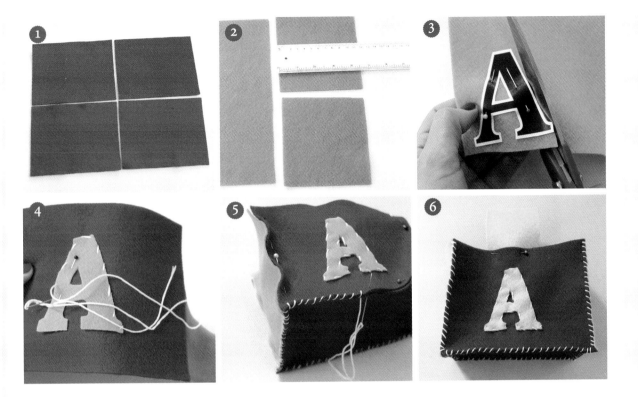

TO MAKE THE INITIAL

4. On the sheet of paper draw or print out a letter of your choice (use Cambria bold font; point size 290). Carefully cut the paper initial out and pin it onto the remaining section of the end panel sheet of felt. Draw around it and cut it out (*see image 3*).

5. Pin the felt initial onto the centre of the front panel of the bag. Use the embroidery thread and needle to sew it in place (*see image 4*).

TO CREATE THE BAG

6. Pin all 4 sides and the base of the bag together.

7. Using the embroidery thread and needle, sew the bag together using an overcast stitch (*see image 5*).

8. Take the felt handle (*see point 3*) and pin one end onto the inside middle of the front section of the bag. Fold the handle over to meet the back of the bag and attach the free end to the inside middle section of the back of the bag (*see image 6*).

9. Use a running stitch to sew the handle in place with the white embroidery thread.

Children love unhealthy food – that's the nature of the game – but when my kids eat a burger, I'm far happier if I know what's gone into it. The recipes that follow, including the mini burgers, are easy to make, really tasty and are dishes that both kids and adults will enjoy. Especially, the cake …

Panini Soldiers

MAKES: 15–18

INGREDIENTS
400g mozzarella cheese
600g cherry tomatoes
3 large panini baguettes
400g Applewood smoked ham
30g fresh basil leaves

SPECIAL EQUIPMENT
Griddle pan

Place the griddle pan over a medium heat. Thinly slice the mozzarella, then wash and cut the cherry tomatoes in half.

Slice the 3 paninis lengthways and lay 3 halves down on a work surface. Lay 1 slice of ham on each of the halves, then place the mozzarella slices and the tomato on top. Sprinkle with basil leaves.

Sandwich with the remaining panini halves and press gently together with the palm of your hand to push the ingredients together.

Slide the paninis onto the hot griddle and cook for 3 minutes on each side, or until the cheese inside starts to melt and the outside of the sandwich starts to turn golden brown.

Remove from the heat and slice the paninis into 5cm-wide soldiers.

Serving suggestion: Great with French's mustard.

TIP   Use portobello mushrooms instead of ham for another tasty option.

Mini Burgers

MAKES: 24

INGREDIENTS
2 medium white onions,
    finely chopped
3 tsp dried oregano
4 tsp paprika
4 tsp finely chopped fresh
    coriander
2 level tsp freshly ground
    black pepper
2 large pinches of salt
10 tbsp breadcrumbs
800g lean minced beef
2 large eggs
24 mini burger buns
100g bag rocket leaves

Preheat the grill to 200°C or to a medium–high heat.

In a large bowl, mix the chopped onion, oregano, paprika, coriander, black pepper, salt and breadcrumbs. Add in the minced beef and use your hands to make sure the ingredients are fully combined.

In a separate clean bowl, whisk the eggs together. Add the egg a tablespoon at a time to the mince mixture, until it is wet enough to shape into hamburger patties with your hands. Make the patties the size of the mini burger buns.

Put the patties on a wire rack over a baking tray under the preheated grill and cook for 8–9 minutes per side.

Cut the mini burger buns in half and when ready, put one burger in each bun with some rocket leaves.

Serving suggestion: Good with a side bowl of mayonnaise, ketchup or French's mustard.

... *with* Homemade French Fries

SERVES: 8–10

INGREDIENTS
8–10 medium baking
    potatoes, cut into 1cm
    thick strips
2 tbsp olive oil
Salt
Ground black pepper

Preheat the oven to 220°C/Gas 7.

Place the potato chips in a large bowl. Drizzle with olive oil and season to taste with salt and pepper.

Put in a baking tray or roasting tin in the preheated oven and cook for 25 minutes, or until golden brown, turning the fries regularly.

Serving suggestion: Great sprinkled with malt vinegar and served with a side bowl of ketchup or mayonnaise.

The Perfect Triple Chocolate Milkshake

SERVES: 4

INGREDIENTS
600ml full-fat milk,
    chilled
4 tbsp hot chocolate
    powder
500ml good-quality triple
    chocolate dairy
    ice cream

SPECIAL EQUIPMENT
Blender; 4 x 250ml
glass bottles

Place all the ingredients in the blender and blitz for 90 seconds.

Pour into the glass bottles and serve immediately with straws.

Variations

For Strawberry Milkshake

600ml full-fat milk; ½-litre good-quality vanilla ice cream (I use Green & Blacks); 450g strawberries, washed and hulled; 2 bananas; drizzle of strawberry syrup (such as Monin)

Mix as above.

For Vanilla and Banana Milkshake

500ml full-fat milk; 500ml good-quality vanilla ice cream (such as Green and Black's Organic); 2 bananas; 2 tsp vanilla extract

Mix as above.

TIP Serve the milkshakes in pre-used glass bottles.

A *Very* Creamy M&M Chocolate Cake

This pretty and colourful cake is a match made in heaven – M&Ms and cream. What more do little fingers want? It's not something you would want to give your kids every day, but for a birthday it's special enough to make any child happy. The variation 'Coronation Cake' (*pictured on page 125*) is slightly more grown-up, perhaps, but it is based on a delicious cake that I had when I was eight years old, one that I never forgot.

MAKES: 1 cake layer (triple the quantity to make 3 layers, as in photo opposite)

INGREDIENTS
Cake
150g unsalted butter, softened, plus extra for greasing
150g caster sugar
230g self-raising flour
100g good-quality cocoa powder
30ml full-fat milk
3 large eggs
¼ tsp salt

Buttercream
150g unsalted butter, softened
370g icing sugar, sifted
1 tsp vanilla extract
3 tbsp cold water
150g M&M's

SPECIAL EQUIPMENT
20cm-round loose-bottomed cake tin;
parchment paper;
palette knife

Preheat the oven to 190°C/Gas 5. Grease and line the cake tins with the parchment paper.

In the bowl of a free-standing mixer, using the paddle attachment, mix together the butter and sugar until soft, creamy and light in colour. In a separate small bowl whisk the eggs. While the mixer is turning at a slow–medium speed, gradually sift in the flour and cocoa powder and add the milk, eggs and salt.

Continue mixing until the batter is smooth and creamy but don't over mix. Pour the mixture into the lined tin, using a palette knife to spread it out evenly.

Place in the preheated oven and bake for 25–30 minutes or until a knife inserted into the centre of the cake comes out clean. Remove from the oven and allow the cake to cool fully before removing it from its tin. Put on a cake stand or plate ready to be decorated.

To make the buttercream topping and filling, in the bowl of the mixer, use the paddle attachment to mix together the butter and icing sugar. Add the vanilla extract and the water and mix until smooth and combined.

Use the palette knife to spread the buttercream over the top and sides of the cake. Decorate with M&Ms, starting from the outside and working in, press the sweets at regular intervals into the soft icing.

To create a 3-tiered cake, increase the ingredients proportionately by 3. Repeat the above method. Place the second cake on top of the cream-covered bottom layer and spread with cream. Top with the third cake and decorate with M&M's.

Variation

For Coronation Cake

MAKES: 2 cake layers (double quantities to make 4 layers as in photo on page 124)

INGREDIENTS
Cake: 225g caster sugar; 225g unsalted butter, softened; 4 large eggs; 225g self-raising flour, sifted; 2 tbsp full-fat milk; 2 tsp vanilla extract

Filling/topping: 227g clotted cream; 250g icing sugar; 100g unsalted butter, softened; 2 tbsp water; 1–2 drops rose food colouring; 2 tsp Le Sirop de Monin Fraise (strawberry); 200g strawberries, washed and hulled

Preheat the oven to 190°C/Gas 5. Grease and line the cake tins with parchment paper. Follow the method opposite to make the cake batter. Divide the mixture between the 2 lined tins and follow the instructions for baking and cooling.

Use a palette knife to spread the clotted cream over the surface of a layer of sponge. To make the buttercream filling, follow the method opposite, but add rose food colouring and the strawberry syrup instead of vanilla extract. Use a palette knife to spread the buttercream over the second layer of the cake.

A World of Make Believe

Children love make believe and secrecy, special hideaways or corners of the house and garden where they can pretend to be whatever they want, wherever they want, with their friends. And that is what this occasion is all about. It's about creating a simple space outside for young children's imaginations to run riot in; an area in which they can laugh, play, run, and dream – and one, moreover, in which there's not a computer in sight.

It's not hard to do this. Tie a few bunches of balloons to a tree (in your garden or a park) at just above your child's head height. Place the giant toadstools around a picnic table or picnic blanket (such as my 'Laying on the Lawn' quilt; *see pages 52–55*).

Hang paper bunting just above the table and bring out a few giant TV cushions (*see pages 176–79*) for the little people who want to plop down on them, rather than plot world domination in the wigwam.

Before the guests arrive, turn on a bubble machine. The children immediately walk into a world full of bubbles that they can then chase around and pop.

Give the children all these things and some burgers, chips and milkshakes, and I promise you they'll be ever so, ever so happy.

Oh, and a bit of cake, of course.

A Summer Fête

THE ENGLISH SUMMER FÊTE is a glorious tradition. As a child, I would look forward to that August Saturday afternoon when I'd be able to wear my new summer dress and make my way, holding my mum or dad's hand, to the place where the fête was being held. It was the perfect place to spend my pocket money and I developed a fascination with all of the homegrown goodies that seemed to thrive behind the closed doors of my neighbours' homes.

Now, even though I'm all grown up and am taking part in the fête as a stallholder, I look forward to it every bit as much. By the time the day finally dawns the fruit, vegetables and flowers in my back garden have had weeks of warming up in the sun and are ripe for picking. Scented stocks are cut and popped into tiny jam jars before being packaged in upright paper bags. Peas, beans, courgettes and berries all jostle for space in the boot of the car, ready to be unloaded and presented to the world. I also sneak in a some crafty items that I've made specifically for selling.

The following pages give you some of my insider tips and provide guidance on some useful things to make for your stall (such as jams) and how to present them to their best possible advantage. It's true, it's all good fun, but most people with a table at a fête have one because it gives them a splendid opportunity to show off. And why not, for heaven's sake? If you're keen on growing your own fruit and vegetables or simply love the flowers that you've handgrown, then I'm all for showing off. And the summer fête is the perfect opportunity for you to do just that and have a great time to boot!

Cherry Menlove

There is nothing wrong with loading your stall up with crafts. Summer fêtes are often a goldmine of original pieces – and hundreds of cottage industries start up each year from the success of crafts sold at such events. This year I have stuck to making an apron (which I also wear) and a very simple tablecloth with napkins for the crafts on my stall.

A Summertime Apron

The following pages (*pages 135–59*) give instructions on how to assemble this summertime apron in 3 easy stages:

STAGE 1 shows you how to make the apron skirt, frill and waistband.

STAGE 2 shows you how to make the fluted ties, top section and neck loop.

STAGE 3 shows you how to attach the ties and front section to the skirt.

YOU WILL NEED:

- 2m fabric of your choice
- Scissors
- Pins
- 2.5m x 1cm binding
- Sewing cotton
- Sewing machine
- Ruler
- Pencil
- Measuring tape
- Iron and ironing board

STAGE 1

TO MAKE THE APRON'S SKIRT, FRILL AND WAISTBAND

1. Cut a piece of fabric measuring 48cm (l) x 80cm (w) for the apron skirt. Cut 2 strips of binding 45cm long (for the skirt's side edges) and 1 length of 80cm (for the skirt's bottom edge). Pin and iron the binding in place around the 3 edges of the skirt fabric. It should meet at the bottom corners and ends approximately 3cm from the top of the skirt on either side (the sides of the fabric measure 48cm whereas the binding is only cut to 45cm in length) (*see image 1*). Sew in place.

2. Use pins to create 7 evenly spaced pleats 8cm apart from each other along the top of the apron skirt. Each pleat should measure 1.5cm wide. Once the pleats are pinned in place, the width of top edge of the skirt should be 56cm (*see image 2*).

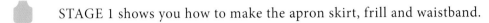

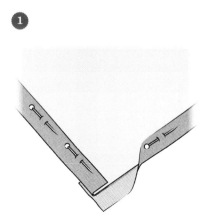

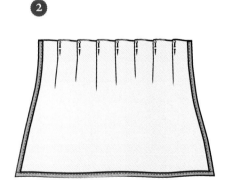

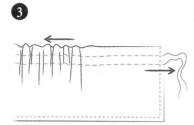

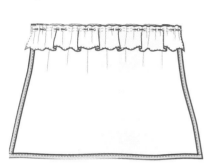

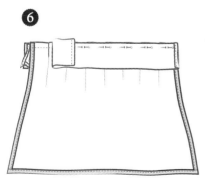

3. From the leftover fabric cut a strip, measuring 110cm (l) x 10cm (w) for the apron frill. Pin a double hem (5mm per hem) in place at both ends and along the bottom edge of the fabric. Sew the hems in place. To create the gathered effect for the frill, 1cm down from the unhemmed top edge of the fabric, use a 3mm-wide stitch to sew 2 rows of stitches. Allow a 1cm gap between the rows. Make sure that there is an excess of sewing cotton at either end of each stitched row. Take 2 pieces of cotton from one side and tie them together into a knot; then take hold of the 2 pieces of cotton at the other end and push the fabric away from you towards the knotted end to create soft gathered folds (see image 3).

4. When the gathered frill measures exactly 56cm, tie the loose pieces of sewing cotton into a knot. Then attach the unhemmed edge of the frill to the top unhemmed edge of the apron skirt. Pin the frill onto the skirt just beneath the gathered folds (see image 4).

5. To create the waistband, from the remaining fabric cut 2 pieces measuring 12cm (l) x 60cm (w). Pin and sew a double hem (1cm per hem) at both ends. After hemming, the length of the waistband strips should be 56cm.

6. Lay one of the waistband strips face down across the top of the unhemmed edge of the skirt. It should also sit on top of the frill that has just been pinned in place. Pin in place along and just under the 2 stitched rows. Sew all 3 layers together, removing the pins as you sew. Fold the waistband fabric back over the right way. This should effectively hide all the unhemmed edges (see image 5).

7. Lay the apron skirt face down on a flat surface. Take the second waistband strip and following the process in step 6, pin it face down to the top edge of the apron skirt (see image 6).

8. Sew in place, removing the pins as you do so.

TO MAKE THE FLUTED TIES, TOP SECTION AND NECK LOOP

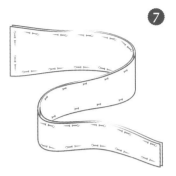

1. To make the fluted ties, from the remaining fabric, cut out 4 strips, measuring 105cm (l) x 15cm (w). Lay them out on a flat surface. Use a ruler and a pencil to draw the tie shape of the tie onto the fabric. Each tie should taper down from 15cm, at one end, to 7cm, at the other. These measurements make it 'fluted'.

2. Take 2 of the fluted pieces of fabric, pin them together face to face (5mm in from the edge). Leave the narrow end unpinned (*see image 7*).

3. Sew the 3 pinned edges together, removing the pins as you do so. Then turn the right way out and iron flat.

4. Repeat this step to make the second tie.

5. To create the apron's top section, cut out another piece of fabric measuring 35cm (l) x 30cm (w). Cut out 2 strips of binding, each measuring 35cm. Pin the binding to the 2 x 35cm sides of the apron top (*see image 8*). Sew and iron the binding in place.

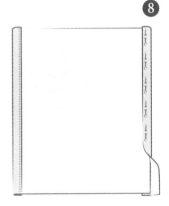

6. Cut another piece of fabric measuring 48cm (l) x 10cm (w) for the apron's neck loop. Fold it in half lengthways, pattern-side in. Allowing for a 1cm hem, pin along the outer edge but leave the 2 ends open (*see image 9*). Sew in place, removing all the pins.

7. Turn the fabric back the right way and iron flat. Take one end of the neck loop and pin it (1cm from the end of the neck loop fabric) to the back of one side of the top edge of the apron top. Repeat this step with the remaining end of the neck loop at the other end of the apron top.

8. Cut a 30cm length of binding. Pin the binding along the top edge of the apron's top section thus covering the ends of the neck loop at either side. To make sure that the neck loop is secured in place, along with the binding, fold the neck loop over the top of the binding (*see image 10*). This makes both the neck loop and the binding more secure. Pin together and sew in place.

STAGE 3

TO ATTACH THE TIES AND TOP SECTION TO THE SKIRT

1. Take one of the waistband ties and pin the unhemmed end to the inside of the back of the waistband, approximately 5cm in from the outside edge (*see image 11*). Pin in place. Repeat this step with the other waistband tie.

2. Leave an opening of 30cm at the top of the waistband, wide enough to accommodate the apron top. Position the apron top in the middle of the waistband and tuck it into the band approximately 4–5cm inside. Pin into place (*see image 12*). Sew along the top of the waistband 2–3mm in from the top.

3. Finally, sew along the sides of the waistband, encasing and securing the ties in between the waistband itself (*see image 13*).

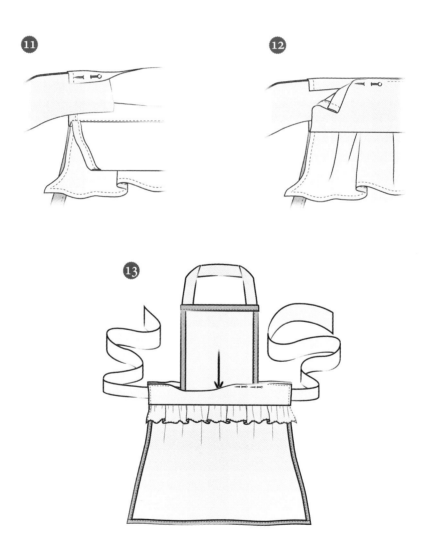

Simple Summer Tableware

These simple but stylish napkins and the tablecloth were made from leftover material in my fabric stash. The napkins can be sold individually or tied together with some hessian or a pretty ribbon and sold as mismatching sets.

YOU WILL NEED:

- Assorted fabrics
- Measuring tape
- Pencil
- Scissors (paper/fabric)
- Pins
- Sewing cotton
- Iron and ironing board

NOTE: Napkins come in various sizes. The instructions relate to 54cm x 54cm squares. Please adjust your sizing accordingly.

TO MAKE A NAPKIN

1. Cut out the napkin fabric to measure 58cm x 58cm. Fold and pin a double hem (1cm per hem) along all four sides.

2. Sew the double hem in place.

3. Iron the napkins flat. Tie in batches with string or pretty ribbon.

TO MAKE A TABLECLOTH

1. Measure the width and length of your table (or choose a standard size if you're making it to sell). Add another 20–25cm to each measurement to allow a practical drop. Use these measurements to cut out the tablecloth from a piece of fabric of your choice.

2. Fold and pin a double hem (1cm per hem) along all 4 sides.

3. Sew the double hem in place and iron flat.

Summertime is a very busy time of year in my kitchen. I feel like I'm racing against the clock to get the most from my garden's produce. The summer garden's best friend, the freezer, really comes into its own as I freeze the glut of produce, enabling me to use it later in the year. My favourite way of using fruit and veg is to make jams, preserves and chutneys, also perfect for selling at the summer fête. In the following pages, 143–47, I provide you with checklists, tips and some much-used jam recipes.

Jam-making Checklist

Preserving is much easier than you think if you're prepared. Following is a checklist of essential equipment, some handy tips and also a template for a jam jar label that can be used once you've made the recipes that follow. All my jams will keep for up to 6 months unopened in a store cupboard. Once opened, refrigerate and use within a month.

ESSENTIAL EQUIPMENT

- 9-litre preserving pan or large heavy-based saucepan (avoid aluminium)
- Long-handled wooden spoon
- Potato masher

- Funnel
- Jelly bag and stand set
- Empty glass jam jars with lids/ Le Parfait airtight jars (500ml)
- Jam jar label (*see below*)

- Wax paper preserving discs (if jars do not have a rubber seal)

HOW TO STERILISE YOUR JARS

Wash the jars and lids well in hot soapy water. Place the jars and lids on the shelf of a low-heated oven for 10 minutes. Remove them using tongs.

When using Le Parfait jars, follow the above instructions, but remove the rubber rings beforehand. Immerse the rings in boiling water then leave to dry.

JAM JAR LABEL TEMPLATE
(can also be used to attach to a bottle of berry vodka and other gifts)

Strawberry Jam

MAKES: 4 x 212ml jars

INGREDIENTS
950g fresh strawberries,
  washed and hulled
450g granulated sugar
450g jam/preserving sugar
Juice of 4 lemons

Put 225g of the strawberries and 225g of granulated sugar in the pan. Over a low heat, use a potato masher to turn the fruit and sugar to a pulp. Simmer for 5–6 minutes, stirring continuously. Add the remaining strawberries, the rest of both sugars and lemon juice. Stir gently for about 12 minutes, until the sugar has dissolved. Bring the jam to the boil and cook for a further 12 minutes, stirring regularly. Test the jam for setting (*see tip*). Once the setting point has been reached, take the pan off the heat immediately. Pour the jam through a funnel into the sterilised jars. Immediately place wax discs on top before screwing on the lids (if not Le Parfait jars). Allow to cool and label the jars. Store in a cool, dark place until ready to use.

TIP

To test the setting point, put a plate in the freezer for 10 minutes. Remove and put a spoonful of jam onto the plate. After a minute, push the jam with your finger. If it wrinkles, then your jam is set. if it hasn't set, keep testing like this every 2–3 minutes.

Cherry Jam

MAKES: 2 x 350ml jars

INGREDIENTS
800g cherries, pitted
420g jam/preserving sugar
400g granulated sugar
Juice of 3 lemons

Put 200g granulated sugar and 260g cherries in the pan. Over a low heat, use a potato masher to gently squash the cherries, but do not mash them.

Simmer the mixture very gently for 5–6 minutes, stirring. Add the remaining cherries, both sugars and lemon juice and stir well. Leave the fruit to simmer over a low heat for 30 minutes.

Remove the pan from the heat and test for setting (*see tip*). If the setting point has been reached, pour the jam through a funnel into sterilised jars. If you are not using Le Parfait jars, then immediately place wax discs on top before screwing on the lids. Allow to cool and label the jars. Store in a cool, dark place until ready to use.

Serving suggestion: Chill before serving. It tastes better!

Peach Conserve

MAKES: 2 x 350ml jars

INGREDIENTS
1.5kg fresh peaches
   (about 12 ripe peaches)
Zest of 1 lemon
Juice of 2 lemons
700g granulated sugar
200ml liquid pectin

Place the peaches in a large bowl of boiling water. Leave to soak for about 5 minutes, or until the skins start to split. Then put in a large bowl of cold water. Peel the skins from the peaches and remove the stones. Cut the peaches into small pieces and put them in the pan along with the lemon zest. Over a low heat, let the fruit soften for 4–5 minutes. Stir with a wooden spoon.

Mix in the lemon juice and sugar and gently mash the fruit with a potato masher. Bring to the boil, turn the heat down and let the mixture simmer for around 20–5 minutes. Stir in the pectin. Remove the pan from the heat and test if the setting point has been reached (*see tip, page 144*). Once set, pour through a funnel into the sterilised jars. Immediately place wax discs on top before screwing on the lids (if not using Le Parfait jars). Allow to cool and label the jars. Leave in a dark, cool place until ready to use.

Classic Redcurrant Jelly

MAKES: 2 x 350ml jars

INGREDIENTS
800g fresh redcurrants,
   washed and stems
   removed
125ml cold water
800g granulated sugar
Juice of 1 lemon
200ml liquid pectin
700g granulated sugar

SPECIAL EQUIPMENT
Jelly bag/stand

Put the redcurrants and water in the pan. Bring slowly and gently to the boil over a medium heat. Lower the heat and simmer for 10 minutes, stirring the fruit carefully. If you stir too briskly, this can cause the jelly to cloud later. Add the sugar and lemon juice and turn the heat up. Allow the mixture to boil for 15 minutes, until all the sugar has dissolved. Then stir in the pectin. Again, be gentle with the fruit during the boiling process and don't burn the fruit. Skim off any scum that develops and take the pan off the heat. Test the setting point (*see tip, page 144*).

Once the setting point is reached, place the jelly bag/stand or sieve over a large bowl. Pour the contents of the pan through the sieve. Leave for 6–8 hours, or preferably overnight, to allow the redcurrant juices to filter through. Pour the jelly through the funnel into sterilised jars. Place wax discs on top of the jelly before screwing on the lids. Label the jars. Leave in a dark, cool place until use.

Buttery Scones with Jam and Cream

There's nothing more British than fresh buttery scones with a pot of homemade jam and a big dollop of clotted cream. Mmm.

MAKES: 4 large scones

INGREDIENTS
50g unsalted butter,
    softened, plus extra
    for greasing
220g self-raising flour
Salt
20g caster sugar
135ml full fat milk
1 large egg, beaten
Homemade strawberry jam,
    to serve
Clotted cream, to serve

SPECIAL EQUIPMENT
6cm round cookie cutter

Preheat the oven to 190°C/Gas 5. Lightly grease a baking tray.

Sift the flour and salt into a large bowl. Add the butter and use your fingertips to rub it into the flour to create a crumbly mixture. Then mix in the sugar and pour in the milk. Continue mixing the ingredients together using your fingertips, until you have a soft dough.

Turn the dough out onto a well-floured work surface and knead it for about 20 seconds. Shape the dough into a ball. Place in a clean bowl and chill for 20 minutes.

Remove the dough from the fridge and, on a well-floured work surface, use the palm of your hand to pat the dough out flat to a thickness of about 2.5cm.

Use the cookie cutter to cut 4 circles out of the dough. Place them on the baking tray. Brush the tops of the scones with the beaten egg.

Place in the preheated oven and bake for 15–20 minutes, or until the scones have risen and are golden brown.

Serving suggestion: Perfect with just butter, but even better with a lot of clotted cream and some strawberry jam (*see page 144*).

Blackcurrant Vodka

MAKES: 1-litre bottle

INGREDIENTS
½ vanilla pod, split
    open lengthways
100g caster sugar
Juice of ½ lemon
500g blackcurrants
500ml bottle of vodka
    (I use Smirnoff 80 Proof
    Red Vodka)

SPECIAL EQUIPMENT
Food or cake net; funnel;
jelly bag/stand; fine sieve

In a large bowl, combine the the vanilla pod, sugar, lemon and black-currants. Cover with the food net and leave for 2–3 minutes, allowing the fruit mixture to macerate. Mash the berries gently.

Pour the fruit mixture through the funnel into a sterilised 1-litre bottle. Add 250ml of vodka. Seal the bottle tightly and chill in the fridge for a week.

Remove the bottle and pour the contents through the bag of the jelly stand, allowing the juices to drain through into the bowl below. Pour the juice from the bowl through the sieve into another clean bowl.

Use the funnel or jug to pour about 400ml of liquid into a sterilised 1-litre bottle. Top with the rest of the vodka. Seal the bottle and shake well.

Serving suggestion: Neat with plenty of ice. Or add lemonade to make a drink that's a bit more mellow and far less potent!

TIP For a great gift, use the jam jar label template on page 143 to create a personalised gift tag on pretty card. Tie to the bottle with raffia or a ribbon.

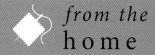

Setting Up Your Stall

When planning your stall, think about it from a visitor's perspective. Add personal touches so that people can get a real feel for the love and care that has gone into creating that pot of homemade jam, for example. Be proud of what you're selling and visitors and customers alike will pick up on your enthusiasm. Here are a few tips to help you set up your stall:

- **PERSONALISE**
  Add personalised printed labels to jars (*see page 143*). Write or draw on them – or cut out and glue on images that you particularly like.

- **PACKAGING**
  Go that extra mile. Make up boxes of homegrown fruit and vegetables. Pick lovely flowers from the garden and sell them in a crate or trug. Not only will you sell more, but people will love the fact that they can keep the trug or box forever.

- **PRESENTATION**
  Presentation is everything. Use different levels and heights to show off your goodies. I placed an old stepladder by my table and put various jars of jams and fruit pots on the steps. Shelves, no matter how rickety or old, can also showcase craft items, linens, and so on. Similarly, a washing line strung up behind your table with goods pegged to it, or hung over it, can show off tablecloths and napkins to perfection.

DECORATION AND SETTING
- Decorate your stall with bunting, potted plants and vases of cut flowers. Stamp your personality on it. Also, don't forget your car. It's a useful resource. If there is room, then park right next to your table. Reverse in, open the boot and sell out of there, too!

RELAX
- Make your customers as comfortable as possible: don't intimidate them by hovering over them. Stand *behind* your table. People will feel more comfortable browsing, if they're not worried about being forced into buying something.

A Bank Holiday
Barbecue

IT'S LATE ON A THURSDAY AFTERNOON and I hear on the radio that the weather over the last bank holiday weekend of the year is going to be amazing! It seems that the mercury is going to rise for the last time this summer, and I am absolutely determined to make the most of it.

None of my friends have any firm plans because nobody expected the weather to be this gorgeous and, since we just *have* to take advantage of this unexpected blessing, I immediately invite everyone over for the last barbecue of the season, a bit of grown up fun in the sun.

Everyone can make it so this gives me a day-and-a-half to plan, make best friends with some delicious meat and fish marinades and stock up on those all essential barbecue coals and beers.

These last-minute gatherings are great as they don't require everything to be absolutely perfect. They're all about relaxing in an informal setting. So, the pressure's off as it's all about good company, good food, some comfy seats and great tunes. That's really all you need.

… Oh, and those final rays of summer sun, of course.

from the
craft room

The crafts in this chapter are all about making the people who come to your house feel welcome. The deck chair is simple and stylish and, crucially, very comfy, too! The menu board is useful at any time of the year. Simply hang it from your garden gate or over the makeshift bar with a handwritten message on. Alternatively, prop it by the barbecue and write the menu on it.

STEP by STEP

A Summer Deck Chair Cover

YOU WILL NEED:

- 1 deck chair
- Fabric (3m x 50cm; or 2 different fabrics, 1.5m x 50cm each)
- Scissors
- Pins
- Sewing cotton
- Sewing machine
- Upholstery pins
- Hammer

NOTE: This is based on my deck chair which measured: 46cm (total seat width) x 82cm (frame height). Adjust the measurements for your own chair, if necessary.

TO MAKE THE COVER

1. Remove the old cover from the deck chair, leaving just the wooden frame (*see image 1, right*).

2. Cut 2 pieces of fabric, measuring 120cm (l) by 45cm (w). Place them pattern-side in, face to face. Pin the fabric pieces together along both sides and along the bottom edge, then pin the top opening closed, leaving a gap of 25cm in the middle to allow room for the cover to be turned the right way out (*see image 2, right*). Sew together, 2cm in from the edge. Cut any excess fabric from the corners and then turn the cover the right way out (*see image 3, right*).

3. Take the partly open end of the seat cover and fold the top and bottom edges of the fabric inwards by 2cm. Iron the fabric flat for the neatest finish. Pin the open edge closed and sew a border 1.5 cm from the edge along all 4 sides using a running stitch (*see image 4, right*).

TO ATTACH TO THE DECK CHAIR

4. Erect the frame and lay it face down on the ground so the top end is closest to you. Wrap one end of the fabric around the top of the deck chair and hammer the upholstery pins securely and evenly spaced into place on the underside of the wooden frame (*see image 5, right*). Repeat at the other end of the chair frame (*see image 6, right*).

A Simple Message Board

YOU WILL NEED:

- Picture frame
- Measuring tape
- Pencil
- Handsaw
- MDF, cut to the same size as the picture frame
- Newspaper
- 250ml tin blackboard paint
- Small paintbrush
- Duct tape
- Chalk

1. Measure the inside width and length of the picture frame. Draw to size onto the MDF (*see image 1, right*).

2. Use a handsaw to cut the MDF piece (*see image 2, right*). It should fit inside the frame.

3. Lay the newspaper out on a flat surface. Place the MDF on top and paint one side of the MDF evenly with the blackboard paint (*see image 3, right*). Leave to dry as per the instructions on the tin. Repeat the process so that the MDF has three even coats of paint.

4. When dry, place the blackboard back in to the picture frame and secure in to the frame using heavy-duty duct tape. Before the party, carefully write out your welcome message or menu (*see image 4, right*).

TIP This message board is handy in the kitchen for mesages to your loved ones or simply for jotting down a shopping list.

The recipes in this section are all about sharing food in a relaxed and informal setting. They involve creating huge plates and bowls piled high with juicy ribs, tasty salads and corn, straight from the garden. Some chilled beer, along with a bowl of punch and some homemade lemonade (*see pages 184–85*) are all we need to drink. And, the result is that friends and family can have a great time eating tasty food, with their fingers if they want, while turning their faces up to catch the last of the year's sun.

Summer Red Pepper and Spanish Chorizo Salad

SERVES: 8–10

INGREDIENTS
2 tbsp chilli oil
5 medium garlic cloves, thinly
    sliced
2 tbsp olive oil, plus a little
    extra for frying
800g white farmhouse loaf,
    cut into 2–3cm cubes
8 red bell peppers, cut into
    thin strips
675g Spanish chorizo,
    thinly sliced
8 spring onions, thinly sliced

Over a medium heat, add 1 tablespoon of chilli oil to a large non-stick frying pan. Gently fry the garlic for 3–4 minutes, until it has softened.

Add 2 tablespoons of olive oil, the rest of the chilli oil and the cubed bread to the pan. Fry for 3–5 minutes, or until the bread has turned golden on all sides. Stir constantly so it doesn't stick or burn. The bread absorbs oil quickly so add a mixture of both oils if it seems too dry. Remove from the pan and transfer to a large bowl.

Cook the peppers and chorizo slices in the frying pan, over a low heat for 4–5 minutes, until softened.

Mix the chorizo and pepper in with the bread. Finally, mix in the sliced spring onions.

Serving suggestion: Transfer to a large serving plate. To finish, tear up about 180g of fresh parsley and sprinkle over the top of the dish.

Flaked Almond and Chickpea Couscous Salad with Pomegranate, Olives and Feta

This salad is fantastic for vegetarians and non-vegetarians alike. This also makes a quick light lunch for work or the basis of a simple supper with friends.

SERVES: 8–10

INGREDIENTS
1 litre boiled water
500g couscous
400g flaked almonds
2 x 410g tins chickpeas
2 tsp paprika
200g pomegranate seeds
   (about 2 large omegranates)
500g jar pitted green olives
400g feta cheese, crumbled

NOTE: You can, of course, use dried chickpeas, cooked according the instructions on the packet. If you use tins, depending on the brand, you may need to warm the chickpeas through after draining them in order to soften them before adding them to the couscous.

In a large bowl, pour the water over the couscous. Cover with a plate and leave to stand for about 10 minutes. The grains should absorb all the water and appear fluffy and soft to the taste. Use a fork to fluff them up.

In a frying pan, over a medium heat, dry fry the almond flakes for 2–3 minutes, making sure they don't burn.

Drain and rinse the chickpeas. Mix them into the couscous, along with the flaked almonds.

Add the paprika, pomegranate seeds, crumbled feta cheese and green olives and mix well.

Serving suggestion: Drizzle chilli oil into the bowl and mix together one last time before serving.

TIP When using this quick method to cook couscous, it's usually one part couscous to two parts hot water (if preferred, follow the packet instructions).

Tasty Barbecue Ribs

SERVES: 8 (3 ribs each)

INGREDIENTS
2.5kg pork spare ribs
   (about 24 ribs)
250ml water
150ml sunflower oil

Marinade
4 tbsp dark soy sauce
4 tbsp light soy sauce
4 tbsp oyster sauce
4 tbsp rice wine (Mirin)
4 tsp toasted sesame oil
2 tsp sugar
8 fat cloves of garlic, sliced
8 spring onions, washed and
   trimmed
2 red chillies, deseeded
5cm fresh root ginger, grated

Preheat the oven to 150°C/Gas 2.

Make the marinade first. In a medium-sized bowl, mix the soy sauces, oyster sauce, rice wine, sesame oil, sugar, garlic, spring onions, chilli and ginger and use a hand-held blender to mix it thoroughly then set to one side.

Place the uncooked ribs in a large roasting tin and pour in the water. Seal tightly with tin foil and put in the preheated oven for an hour, or until the ribs are tender, but the meat is not falling off the bone.

Transfer the ribs into a large dish or bowl. While still warm, pour both the marinade and the sunflower oil over, making sure that they coat the ribs.

When the ribs have cooled, cover the dish with cling film and put in the fridge for at least 2 hours – or overnight, if you have the time.

Remove from the fridge just before cooking. Place the ribs onto a clean plate and allow any liquid to drain off.

Cook the ribs for 15–20 minutes over a very hot barbecue (the coals should glow white), turning regularly.

TIP   The marinade is also delicious with chicken pieces.

Chilli and Garlic Prawns

MAKES: 20 skewers

INGREDIENTS
50ml sunflower oil
800g King prawns
   (about 100 individual)

Chilli marinade
2 red chillies, deseeded
   and finely chopped
Juice of 6 limes
4 tbsp toasted sesame oil
2 tbsp sesame seeds
6 fat cloves garlic
80g fresh coriander

Soak 20 wooden barbeque skewers in plenty of cold water. Set aside.

Make the marinade first. In a blender, mix the chillies, lime juice, sesame oil, sesame seeds, garlic and half of the coriander. Blend for 10 seconds.

Pour the marinade into a large bowl, then mix in the sunflower oil. Stir in the prawns, making sure that they are evenly coated.

Put a lid over the bowl or cover with cling film. Place in the fridge and leave to marinade for at least an hour prior to barbecuing.

Push 5 prawns on to each skewer and cook for 15 minutes over a very hot barbecue (the coals should glow white), turning regularly.

Garnish with the leftover coriander and serve immediately.

A Corn on the Cob Tower

MAKES: 20

INGREDIENTS
20 corn on the cob, dehusked
1 tsp salt

Garlic butter
125g salted butter
3 garlic cloves
20g fresh flat-leaf
    parsley, chopped

Using a very large saucepan or soup pan, salt the water and boil. Add the corn and cook for about 10–15 minutes, or until tender. Remove and drain the corn and keep warm.

In a saucepan, melt the butter over a low heat. Be careful not to burn it. Mince the garlic cloves. In a medium-sized bowl, mix the garlic with the melted butter and parsley.

Take a large plate or platter and lay a row of corn down. Lay another row of corn on top. Repeat this, until all the corn is used up, and you have created a tower.

Spoon or drizzle the garlic butter over the corn tower.

Serving suggestion: Sprinkle with 2 teaspoons of ground black pepper. They are best served warm.

A Fitting Send-off to Summer

The perfect barbecue for me involves my guests doing little more than lounging on deck chairs by the bar or being able to reach out for a beer from the beer bath. The latter is easy to create. You just need an enamel bowl, a bucket, or a clean dustbin – depending on how many people you are inviting – packed with so much ice that when you stick the beer bottles in (and a litre or so of soda water), they are almost completely submerged. I can promise you will never have a beer colder than from a beer bath.

For decoration, I go for simple, light and breezy. This is a fairly impromptu gathering so shouldn't be expensive. A couple of packets of balloons in soft pastel colours are blown up and tied to a piece of wire that I've stretched over the table, tying it to the pergola and a piece of trellis. A spare piece of checkered fabric thrown over my potting bench turns it into a makeshift bar.

I always have a stash of washed glass food jars, which I bring out to the table and fill with flowers cut from the garden. Cornflowers, cosmos, roses and dahlias are lovely and really do sing for their supper.

My giant TV cushions (*see pages 176–79*) and 'Laying on the Lawn' quilt (*see pages 52–55*) supplement the seating. And every single white lantern, paper candle bag, candlestick and string of fairy lights I can find in the house is put or strung up outside, thus providing a fantastic setting for the great food and some great music, which my brother-in-law provides.

This is a send-off that summer just won't forget, and neither shall we.

Early Autumn Evenings *Around* the TV

NOT EVERYTHING ENJOYABLE OR SOCIABLE has to be a special event or 'occasion'. Some of my best memories come from evenings spent in with friends in my first home, just sitting around, chatting and watching TV. Later, at drama school, a group of us stayed up to watch the Oscars in my flat. We'd shout at the TV if someone didn't deserve to win – or was simply wearing a really hideous dress.

Even today, all these years later, there's nothing more cosy or enjoyable than lounging at home on an early autumn evening, eating popcorn and watching a good movie with my loved ones, particularly if it's a favourite – of which I have so many (*see page 186*).

The following pages are all about downtime, those evenings when you just kick off your shoes, curl up on a sofa or lounge about on giant cushions and enjoy the company of some good friends who've popped over to watch a big game, a movie or to cheer on their favourite celebrity on *Strictly Come Dancing*. All I need to do is provide the essential 'three Ps' – 'Pizza, Popcorn and Punch', while we watch the big screen.

Spending time around the TV might not be as glamorous as taking afternoon tea, but it should be just as vital. We need other people and we need that precious downtime to relax, have fun and scream at the screen. It's a basic ritual and a truly essential part of home life.

I'm a little bit in love with these giant TV cushions, not just because they are part of our TV evenings, but because they can be used for any occassion. I have put my baby twins on them after a bath; I have thrown them onto the lawn when we needed some sun and couldn't be bothered to drag out the garden chairs (the cushions are much more comfy, anyway) and I have taken them to the beach and on picnics.

STEP *by* **STEP**

Giant TV Cushions

MAKES: 1 cushion (*90cm x 90cm with 38cm flap*)

YOU WILL NEED:
- 1 cushion pad (90cm x 90cm)
- 3 different fabric prints (1.5m x 1m each)
- Scissors
- Pins
- Sewing cotton
- Sewing machine
- Iron/ironing board
- 2 x 5cm buttons
- Ruler
- Pencil
- Seam picker/ripper

NOTE: If the cushion pad used is a different size, adjust your measurements accordingly.

TO MAKE THE FRONT OF THE CUSHION

1. Cut a strip, measuring 100cm (l) x 34cm (w), from each of the 3 fabric pieces. Place the fabric lengths face down, side by side on a flat surface. Pin together the 2 inner seams, allowing for a 2cm hem. The overall size of the front section of the cushion at this point should measure 100cm x 94cm (*see image 1, right*). Sew the 2 seams together and iron the seams out flat.

2. Lay the front section out, pattern-side down. Along the bottom edge create a double hem by first folding the fabric over by 2cm and then by 5cm. Pin this hem 4cm from the top edge. Sew in place (*see image 2, right*).

TO MAKE THE BACK OF THE CUSHION

3. Repeat steps 1–2 to create the back section of the cushion, making sure that each of the 3 strips measures 140cm (l) x 34cm (w). The back section will be 40cm longer than the front. Pin and sew a 2cm hem along the 94cm-raw edge of the back section. Lay the front section of the cushion face down on top of the back section. Line the bottom edges up and pin them in place. Then pin the 2 sides of the cover 2cm in from the edge (*see image 3, right*).

TO CREATE THE FLAP

4. Fold the extra 38cm of fabric from the back section over to lie on top of the front section. Pin the outer edges of this flap to the outer seams of the front section (*see image 4*).

5. Sew in place 2cm from the sides. The oversized flap will hold the cushion in place.

TO ATTACH THE BUTTONS AND MAKE BUTTONHOLES

6. While the cover is still inside out, make 2 pencil marks 20cm up from the bottom edge of the inner flap and 30cm in from each side. This is the where the buttons will be positioned.

7. Once the buttons are sewn in place on the front, turn the cushion cover the right way out.

8. On the front flap of the cushion, mark in pencil where the buttonholes will be positioned. The best way to gauge the length of the buttonhole is to add the height of the button to the thickness of the button. The area in between these 2 lines is where the buttonhole needs to go. Using a ruler, draw a faint line on top of the fabric for the buttonholes.

9. Set the sewing machine to create a small tight zigzag stitch. Using the pencil line as a guide sew 2 tight lines, very close together and running parallel with one another. Run the zigzag stitch across the top and bottom of the lines. This seals the edges of the buttonhole.

10. Use a seam picker/seam ripper to gently tear the fabric apart between the 2 parallel lines of zigzag stitching (*see image 5*).

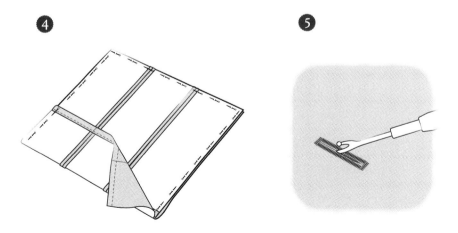

All of the recipes in this section can be prepared ahead of time because you don't want to be stuck making food all night, while everyone else is having fun. It's junk food with a homemade twist and the emphasis is on the three 'Ps' – pizza, popcorn and punch.

TV Pizza

MAKES: 14 mini pizzas

INGREDIENTS
Base
7g sachet fast-action yeast
300ml warm water
1 tsp salt
1 tsp sugar
2 tbsp olive oil
500g strong white bread flour,
    sifted, plus extra for
    kneading

Topping
4 garlic cloves, crushed
300ml passata sauce
400g fresh spinach
Drizzle of olive oil
375g buffalo mozzarella, sliced
2 medium red onions,
    thinly sliced
260g Spanish chorizo ring,
    thinly sliced
100g bag of rocket

SPECIAL EQUIPMENT
Parchment paper

Preheat the oven to 220°C/Gas 7. Line a large baking tray with the parchment paper. Empty the yeast into a small bowl, add the warm water and stir. Put the yeast into the bowl of a free-standing mixer and add the salt, sugar, olive oil and flour.

Use the hook attachment to mix the ingredients together for 7–10 minutes, until they form a ball. Sprinkle some flour on top of the dough ball and cover the bowl with a clean damp tea towel. Leave in a warm place for 1 hour, or until the dough has doubled in size.

Remove the risen dough ball from the bowl and knead for 7–8 minutes on a well-floured surface. Use the free-standing mixer with the dough hook for 3–4 minutes if you don't want to do this by hand. Divide the dough into 14 balls, each about the size of a plum. Roll the balls out into rounds, each measuring 1cm thick by 12cm wide. Place them onto the baking tray. You may need to bake them in batches.

In a large bowl, mix together the crushed garlic and passata. Take a heaped tablespoon and evenly spread it over each pizza base. In a large pan, over a low heat, wilt the spinach with a drizzle of olive oil for 2 minutes. Set aside. Place 2 slices of the mozzarella and the red onion on each pizza. Top with 5 slices of the thinly sliced chorizo and the wilted spinach.

Place in the preheated oven and bake the pizzas for 14–15 minutes. Top with fresh rocket before serving.

Variations

The passata and garlic mix is a great base for other toppings. I regularly use one or several of the following: crumbled feta cheese; sliced spicy sausage; honey-baked ham; finely sliced mushrooms; tiny broccoli florets; slices of red and green pepper; and strips of barbecue chicken.

TIP Make extra dough for more pizzas and keep it for up to a week in the fridge, for use in school lunch boxes or for a weekday supper.

Paprika Popcorn

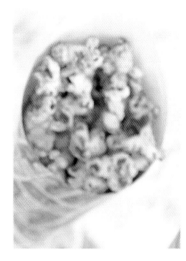

Heat the sunflower oil in a large heavy-bottomed saucepan, over a medium heat, for 1–2 minutes, or until the oil starts to spit. Drop the popping corn in and cover with a tight-fitting lid. Let the corn pop for 3–4 minutes. Shake regularly to make sure the corn doesn't stick to the bottom of the pan. When the popping subsides, remove the pan from the heat.

In a small saucepan, over a low heat, melt the butter. Pour the butter over the popcorn in the large pan and replace the lid. Shake well to ensure that the popcorn is evenly coated in butter.

In a small bowl mix the oregano, sweet smoked paprika and salt. Sprinkle the mix over the buttered popcorn, replace the pan lid and shake well for about 20 seconds. Transfer the popcorn into the cones (*see opposite*), or put in a large serving bowl and eat.

SERVES: 4

INGREDIENTS
1–2 tbsp sunflower oil
100g popping corn
60g slightly salted butter
1½ tsp dried oregano
½ tsp sweet smoked paprika
¼ tsp salt

Variations

For Cherry's Parmesan Popcorn

1–2 tbsp sunflower oil; 100g popping corn; 100g grated Parmesan cheese

Once the popcorn is ready, sprinkle in the Parmesan. Replace the lid and shake well.

For Sticky Maple Popcorn

1–2 tbsp sunflower oil; 100g popping corn; 2–3 tbsp maple syrup

Once the popcorn is ready, drizzle the maple syrup over the top. Replace the lid and shake well.

For Sweet Toffee Popcorn

1–2 tbsp sunflower oil; 100g popping corn; 3 tbsp toffee sauce

Once the popcorn is ready, drizzle the toffee sauce over the top. Replace the lid and shake well.

... *in* Popcorn Cones

YOU WILL NEED:

- A4 paper, patterned or plain
- Sticky tape
- Decorative buttons/ ribbons/stickers
- Craft glue

Place the paper (landscape) on a flat surface. Starting with the bottom left-hand corner, roll towards the centre of the paper, curving the paper around to the right, but along the bottom of the sheet. Try to make the hole at the bottom of the cone as small as possible and the opening at the top as large as possible, so that it can be filled to the brim with popcorn.

Use sticky tape to secure in place with sticky tape along the seam (add a tiny bit to the bottom to seal the hole if you want). Use craft glue to attach decorative pin buttons, stickers or ribbon to cover the seam. Fill with popcorn.

Old-Fashioned Lemonade

MAKES: about 2 litres

INGREDIENTS
9 lemons
130g granulated sugar
1 litre cold water
Lots of ice!

SPECIAL EQUIPMENT
2-litre jug

Juice 8 lemons and cut the last one into thin slices.

Pour the sugar directly into the jug. Slowly add water, stirring constantly until the sugar has dissolved. Add the freshly squeezed lemon juice and continue to mix together.

Top up the jug with as much ice as it will hold. Throw in lemon slices for decoration and an extra zingy kick.

 TIP You can save old jam jars and use them for transporting and serving lemonade – perfect if you run out of glasses at home.

Strawberry Daiquiri

MAKES: 2 large frozen
Daiquiris

INGREDIENTS
100g fresh strawberries,
    washed and hulled
50ml white rum
30ml strawberry schnapps
    or liqueur
50ml fresh lime juice
1 tbsp caster sugar
125ml cloudy lemonade
3 handfuls ice

SPECIAL EQUIPMENT
Blender or cocktail shaker;
Large glasses

Place the glasses in the freezer to chill.

Place the strawberries in the blender. Add the rum, strawberry
schnapps, lime juice, sugar, lemonade and ice. Put the lid on the
blender and mix for 20–30 seconds, or until the Daiquiri mixture is
smooth in consistency. Pour the Daiquiri mix into the glasses and serve
immediately.

Alternatively use a cocktail shaker. Place the ingredients into the
shaker and bash together with the end of a rolling pin. Put the lid on
and shake the ingredients vigorously. Pour through a strainer into the
chilled glasses.

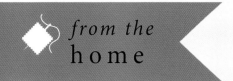

Those Cosy Home Film Nights

Some of the most intimate and heartwarming times of my life have been spent with loved ones watching a fantastic movie … or five. With girlfriends it might be an evening affair, watching a brat pack film, popcorn and punch in hand. With my twins it's different but no less enjoyable – *The Polar Express* on a Saturday afternoon just before Christmas, tree lights twinkling at the end of the room with marshmallows and hot chocolate on tap. The sum of this is, I watch different films for different reasons, but I have 4 categories from which I pull out favourites when the mood takes me. Here they are:

- 'I WISH I LIVED IN 1980s "BRAT PACK" AMERICA'

  Class (1983); *The Outsiders* (1983); *The Breakfast Club* (1985); *St Elmo's Fire* (1985); *The Lost Boys* (1987); *Say Anything* (1989)

- 'INSPIRING ENOUGH TO MAKE A DIFFERENCE'

  One Flew Over the Cuckoos Nest (1975); *Sophie's Choice* (1982); *Silkwood* (1983); *The Color Purple* (1985); *Cry Freedom* (1987); *Good Will Hunting* (1997)

- 'CAN I LIVE IN YOUR HOUSE PLEASE?'

  Father of the Bride (1991); *Practical Magic* (1998); *Hope Floats* (1998); *Something's Gotta Give* (2003); *The Notebook* (2004); *Evening* (2007); *The Women* (2008); *It's Complicated* (2009); *The Blind Side* (2009)

- 'CHRISTMAS TIME MOVIE FEST'

  Meet Me in St Louis (1944); *It's a Wonderful Life* (1946); *When Harry Met Sally* (1989); *Home Alone* (1990); *Toy Story* (1995); *Beautiful Girls* (1996); *You've Got Mail* (1998); *Christmas with the Kranks* (2004); *The Polar Express* (2004)

Halloween

I AM DELIGHTED THAT HALLOWEEN has taken off properly in Britain. In the past, I was always rather jealous of North Americans having this great excuse for a party at the end of October, even if it's just turning cold and everyone's starting to hibernate.

I don't believe Halloween is just about dressing up in extravagant costumes and necking a lot of vodka jelly shots, although it can be that if you like and, in the past, I've also done it that way. Nowadays, however, I much prefer it to be a celebration of good food, with huge amounts of fresh produce and the fantastic opportunity that Halloween allows to decorate the home with my favourite of homegrown garden produce: the pumpkin.

My Halloween palette is not the usual 'pumpkin' orange and black; instead it uses a less traditional blend of ivory, grey and stone. That's not to say that I ignore the traditional side of Halloween; I just incorporate certain elements of it into this colourway that I use. My Halloween wreath, for example, is covered with coloured bats and white fabric pumpkins decorate my home and table (*see pages 194–95*), but, of course, it takes more than lovely decorative features to celebrate Halloween properly.

On a warm October weekend, friends and family gather at our place. If the weather is chilly, we stay warm by the bonfire, made from twigs and wood cleared from the garden. Some people munch on warmed sweet potato and pumpkin doughnuts and Halloween s'mores; others fill up on my beloved nana's hearty beef stew, a dish to warm the coldest of hearts on a wintry Halloween night. Homegrown pumpkins line the walkway to the area where we play quoits and other games. The kids love it, the adults love it and, more importantly, we're all here celebrating this occasion together.

The crafts I have created for this chapter are very much in the style of Halloween, but are made in my favoured lighter decorative palette. The pumpkins can double up as pin cushions; the bat template from the wreath can be used to make tiny bat biscuits or hanging fabric bats and the quoits can be brought out to play, time and time again.

STEP by STEP

Quoits: *A New Take On An Old Game*

Quoits is an ancient game that involves throwing rings from a designated spot to land over or near a spike or pole. Its origin is a matter of dispute, with some people believing that it's derived from the old tradition of throwing horseshoes at a spike in the ground. My version is quite simple and just requires a stretch of grass (about 5m x 2m), a single pole and 4 fabric quoits. The winner is the person who gets the most quoits over the pole. There are 3 rounds in all and, in my game, each person plays as an individual. And the prize, well, the winner gets the largest helping of my spiced apple pudding, and it's *far* too good to share with just anyone …

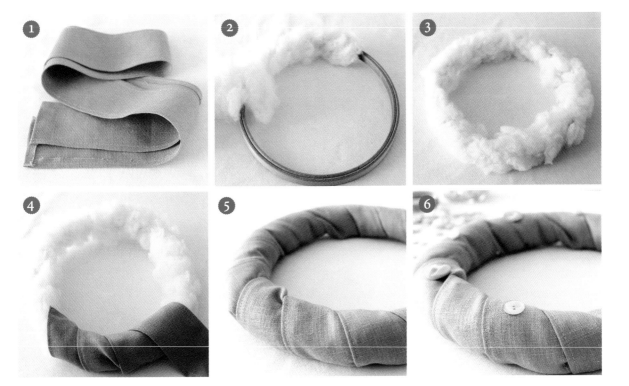

YOU WILL NEED:

- Fabric (1.10m x 1m)
- Measuring tape
- Pencil
- Scissors
- Pins
- Sewing cotton
- Sewing machine
- 4 sewing hoops
  (20cm or 25cm)
- 250g polyester stuffing/
  toy stuffing
- Craft glue
- Selection of buttons,
  for decoration
- 40cm pole/stake

1. Measure and cut the fabric into 8 strips, each measuring 110cm x 8cm
    (*see image 1*). Fold 5mm in from each edge to create a hem on each
    strip. Pin and sew the hems in place.

2. Cover the 4 sewing hoops with the stuffing by gluing it in place (*see
    images 2 and 3*). Take one fabric strip and glue the underside of one
    end to the stuffing. Wind the strip around the stuffing at an angle so
    that the fabric overlaps as it covers the hoop (*see image 4*). Secure the
    end in place with glue. Repeat with the next fabric strip, glueing it into
    place at the point where the last strip of fabric finishes (*see image 5*).

3. Cover the remaining sewing hoops in this way. When finished, glue
    the buttons onto the top of the quoits (*see image 6*). Allow to dry.

    To play: Hammer the pole into the earth to a depth of approximately
    10cm, leaving 30cm above ground. To begin the game, mark out the
    playing area and start throwing …

Fabric Pumpkin

YOU WILL NEED:

Pumpkin

- A4 sheet tracing paper
- Pencil
- Scissors (paper/fabric)
- White felt (25cm x 25cm)
- Pins
- Sewing cotton
- Sewing machine
- Ruler
- Polyester stuffing/ bamboo wadding

Stalk

- Contrasting coloured felt (7cm x 3cm)
- Sewing cotton
- Needle

Optional

- Embroidery thread
- Embroidery needle

TO MAKE THE PUMPKIN BODY

1. Lay tracing paper on the template provided on page 57. Draw around it with a pencil and cut it out. Pin the template to the white felt and trace around it with a pencil. Repeat 5 more times. Cut out the 6 pumpkin shapes (*see image 1, right*).

2. Take 2 of the felt pieces and lay one on top of the other. Line up the edges. Pin to hold in place and then sew along 1 of the curved sides about 5mm from the edge (*see image 2, right*).

3. Pin and sew another section of felt to an open edge of the sewn pieces. Continue to add the pumpkin body a section at a time, making sure that the joins are all facing outwards (*see image 3, right*).

TO MAKE THE STALK

4. Cut a contrasting piece of felt measuring 3cm (l) x 7cm (w). Roll it neatly widthways. Sew the roll together using small, neat stitches. The stalk will be 3cm in length (*see image 4, right*).

TO ASSEMBLE THE PUMPKIN

5. While the pumpkin is still inside out, insert the felt stalk into the top so that about 2cm of the stalk sits inside the pumpkin. Secure by pinning and sewing into place (*see image 5, right*). Remove the pins as you go.

6. Stitch half of the open pumpkin side together. Turn the material the right way out. This will leave 2cm of the stalk on the outside of the pumpkin. Take the stuffing and push it through the open gap. When stuffed, sew the gap closed (*see image 6, right*).

7. To create a realistic pumpkin, use a long needle threaded with cotton and knotted at one end. Push the needle from the base of the stalk, down through the middle of the pumpkin and out the other end, then push it back up again through the base of the stalk. Repeat several times, pulling on the cotton until the pumpkin starts to dip slightly in the middle around the stalk, thus creating a pumpkin shape.

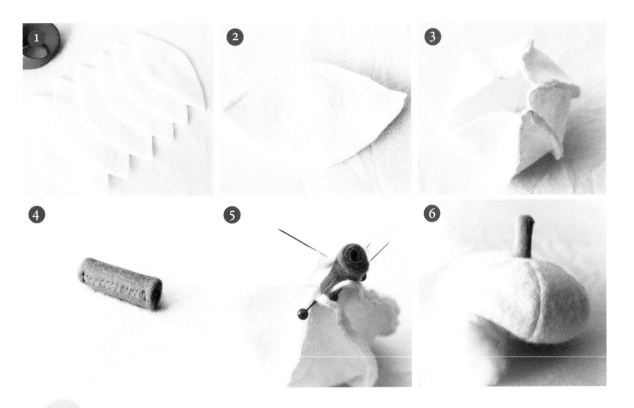

TIP Use as a pin cushion or simply increase the size and use as a table decoration (*see below*).

STEP *by* STEP

Halloween Wreath

YOU WILL NEED:

Wreath

- White felt (1m x 1m)
- Measuring tape
- Pencil
- Scissors (fabric/paper)
- Round straw wreath (38cm x 7cm)
- Hot glue gun

Decoration

- A4 sheet tracing paper
- Selection of coloured felts for to make about 30 bat shapes
- Small piece of card
- Embroidery needle
- White embroidery thread for bat eyes
- Ribbon for hanging (3m x 5cm)

NOTE: This craft suits wreaths of any size, but please adjust your felt quantity accordingly.

TO MAKE THE WREATH

1. Take the white felt and use a ruler to measure out 13 strips, each measuring 22cm x 10cm.

2. Wrap the felt strips around the wreath so that the ends of the strips meet at the back of the wreath. Each of the strips should overlap slightly until the underlying wreath is totally covered.

3. Use a hot glue gun to glue each strip into place at the back.

TO DECORATE THE WREATH

4. Lay the tracing paper on the template below and draw around the bat. Carefully cut it out. Lay the template on a piece of card, draw around it and cut out the bat. Take different pieces of coloured felt and trace around the bat 10 times on each piece of felt. Cut out the felt bats. To make them extra scary use embroidery thread to sew French knots in place for the eyes. Leave a 10cm wide gap at the top of the wreath and hot glue the felt shapes to the front of the wreath.

5. Fill the gap by wrapping the ribbon around the wreath, starting in the middle of the length of ribbon. Leave a length of about 1m on each side for the ribbon to be tied into a bow (*see page 197*). Attach some string or florist wire to the back of the wreath and hang it from a nail on the door or use the ribbon to attach it to a garden post or garden gate.

HALLOWEEN BAT TEMPLATE

Tying a *classic bow*

- Take your chosen length of wide ribbon. In each hand gather up an equal length of material to create two uniform-sized loops, one on each side of the ribbon.

- Cross the right loop over the left. Create a knot by passing the right loop behind the left, then under and up through, all the while making sure that the ribbon is smooth and is not twisted.

- Draw the loops apart so that the ribbon is pulled taut to create a small, neat but loose knot. Adjust the loops so that they are equal in size. Then use your hands to fluff them out.

- With a pair of scissors cut a small inverted 'v' in each tail end.

- Glue or sew it onto your wreath or present or use it to hang your wreath from (*see photo, right, and Christmas Wreath, page 245*).

This occasion takes place in the rather cosy month of October, when the nights are drawing in and comfort food is a must. My nana's beef stew is perfect for this time of year. My nana used to say 'a stew boiled is a stew spoiled' and that's advice I still heed today. For the dish to be just like nana's, with the meat literally falling apart, it has to be slow cooked for several hours. I serve the stew in the garden by the bonfire, for that cosy Autumnal feeling.

My Nana's Beef Stew

SERVES: 8

INGREDIENTS
800g stewing beef, cut into
    2cm cubes
300g smoked back bacon,
    cut into small pieces
1 large white onion, sliced
1 medium leek, sliced
3 medium carrots, sliced
2 large parsnips, sliced
2 x 400g tins chopped
    tomatoes
200ml water
7g bunch fresh thyme
2 beef Oxo cubes
3 tbsp Worcestershire sauce
Salt
Ground black pepper
1 tbsp cornflour

SPECIAL EQUIPMENT
4.2-litre heavy-bottomed
casserole dish

Preheat the oven to 180°C/Gas 4.

Put the beef chunks, bacon pieces and chopped vegetables into the casserole dish. Add the tomatoes (with juice) and pour in the water. Push the bunch of thyme into the middle of the casserole.

Crumble in the stock cubes and add the Worcestershire sauce. Season with salt and pepper to taste. Stir together as best you can.

Place the casserole dish on the hob. Over a low heat, bring to a simmer. Place in the preheated oven with the lid on for 1½ hours.

Then, in a cup, mix the cornflour with a tiny amount of water until it forms a paste. Take the casserole out of the oven and stir in the paste.

Turn the oven down to 150°C/Gas 2 and put the casserole back inside. Bake for another hour. The stew is ready when the meat is so meltingly tender it falls apart.

Serving suggestion: Great with baked potatoes.

Sweet Potato and Pumpkin Doughnuts

As pumpkins are so abundant and are closely associated with Halloween, it seems fitting to make use of them in one of the recipes in this chapter.

MAKES: 20

INGREDIENTS
Doughnuts
250g pumpkin, peeled, deseeded and diced
250g sweet potato, diced
1 tsp salt
½ tsp ground allspice
500g plain flour, plus extra for very ripe pumpkins
7g dried active baking yeast
1 litre vegetable oil

Topping
100g caster sugar
½ tbsp ground cinnamon

SPECIAL EQUIPMENT
Cooking thermometer; straining spoon

Preheat the oven to 140°C/Gas 1.

Bring a large pan of water to the boil. Place the diced pumpkin and sweet potato in the pan and cook gently for 15–20 minutes, or until soft. Drain and then mash until smooth.

Transfer the mixture to a large bowl. Add the salt and ground allspice and mix thoroughly. Stir in the flour and blend until the mixture forms a wet ball. The more ripe the pumpkin, the more flour is necessary to do this.

Pour the yeast into a cup; add a small amount of warm water and stir well. Leave for 10 minutes or until it begins to froth. Pour the yeast into the pumpkin and sweet potato mixture and use your hands to mix it together. Cover the bowl with a clean, damp tea towel and leave in a warm place for 2 hours, or until the dough has doubled in size.

Remove the risen dough from the bowl and divide the dough into 20 evenly sized pieces. Poke your index finger through the middle of each to create the doughnut-shaped hole. If the dough is too sticky to handle, sprinkle more flour onto the pieces.

In a large pan heat the vegetable oil to a temperature of 170°C. Use the cooking thermometer to make sure the temperature is correct. Fry in batches of 4–6 for roughly 3 minutes, or until golden brown, flipping them over once with the straining spoon during that time. Use the straining spoon to remove the doughnuts from the pan and place them on kitchen paper to absorb any excess oil. Transfer to a large ovenproof dish and place in the preheated oven to keep warm.

To make the topping, in a large bowl combine the sugar and cinnamon. Remove the doughnuts from the oven, and while still warm, dip them in the topping mix, coating evenly. Serve warm.

TIP   For a rustic feel fit for Halloween, serve in an old wooden box or crate lined with parchment paper (*see photo, left*).

Spiced Apple Pudding

SERVES: 8–10

INGREDIENTS

Apple filling

6 bramley apples, peeled,
   cored and thinly sliced
30g unsalted butter, plus extra
   or greasing
30g light brown muscovado
   sugar

Topping

60g unsalted butter
60g light brown
   muscovado sugar
½ tsp ground cinnamon
½ tsp ground nutmeg
80g plain flour
60g toasted flaked almonds
3 tbsp water

Pudding mix

200g light brown muscovado
   sugar
200g unsalted butter,
   softened
3 large eggs
250g plain flour
1 tsp ground ginger
½ tsp ground nutmeg
2 tsp ground cinnamon
1 tsp baking powder
100ml buttermilk
2 tbsp almond-flavoured
   liqueur

SPECIAL EQUIPMENT

Loose-bottomed cake tin
(20cm x 10cm); parchment
paper

Preheat the oven to 150°C/Gas 2. Grease the cake tin and line with the parchment paper.

To make the filling, place the sliced apple into a large non-stick saucepan. Add the butter and brown sugar. Heat gently together for 5 minutes, over a low heat, until the apples have softened and have blended well with the butter and sugar. Set aside to cool.

To make the topping, melt the butter over a low heat in a separate non-stick frying pan. Add the sugar, cinnamon, nutmeg, flour, almonds and water and stir for 3–4 minutes with a spoon, until it becomes a crumble-like texture. Remove from heat and set aside.

To make the pudding mixture, in the bowl of a free-standing mixer, use the paddle attachment to cream the sugar and butter, until light and fluffy. Turn the mixer down to its slowest setting and add the eggs one at a time (without beating first). Sift in the flour a tablespoon at a time in between adding in the eggs and mix until combined. Then add the ginger, nutmeg, cinnamon, baking powder and buttermilk and blend together. Pour in the almond liqueur and mix for a few seconds.

Drain any excess juices from the softened apples. Stir them into the pudding batter with a wooden spoon before spooning into the prepared cake tin.

Sprinkle the topping evenly over the top of the pudding mixture. Place in the preheated oven and bake for 1½–1¾ hours, or until a skewer inserted in to the middle comes out almost clean, and the crumbly almond topping has turned brown and crunchy.

Serving suggestion: Great with good-quality vanilla ice cream.

Halloween S'mores

MAKES: 8

INGREDIENTS
32 squares good-quality milk
   chocolate (I use Green &
   Black's)
16 digestive biscuits
40g flaked almonds
16 marshmallows

SPECIAL EQUIPMENT
Bonfire; sticks from the garden
for toasting

NOTE: See pages 26–27
for a recipe for homemade
marshmallows.

Take 4 squares of chocolate and place them on top of a digestive biscuit. Sprinkle a few flaked almonds onto the chocolate.

Poke 2 marshmallows onto the end of a longish stick from the garden. Toast the marshmallows slowly and evenly over the bonfire.

Place the heated marshmallows on top of the chocolate–almond topping.

Make a biscuit sandwich by covering the topping with another digestive biscuit.

The heat from the marshmallows melts the chocolate and creates a gooey soft centre that has you coming back for s'more …

TIP
You can toast the marshmallows in the oven, without the sticks, if you don't have a bonfire to hand!

A Winter Weekend
with Friends

WHEN I HAVE FRIENDS TO STAY for the weekend I see it as an opportunity to give them time off from their normal and sometimes stressful lives. I try to do this by making them feel as welcome and as comfortable in our home as I can. We may just spend hours catching up on the sofa by the fire, with a bottle of Barolo and a few nibbles. Or, I might get up early to put the coffee on in the hope that the smell of a freshly brewed pot will be the first thing they notice when they wake up.

I think that for the weekend to go well I need to give my guests some space of their own yet make them feel entirely comfortable in any corner of my house.

The crafts in this chapter are all focused on the guest bedroom. For this weekend it is their space, not mine or my families, and they need it to be private. I'll organise a couple of trips out to the pub to grab lunch or supper after a day out but the weekend finishes with a hearty Sunday roast before they leave us to head home. I make some loose plans and give my friends the option to go and visit places nearby or simply doze on the sofa with the papers. This weekend is about them, not us, and I want this to be like a stay in a boutique family-run hotel; Hotel Home.

from the
craft room

The three crafts that follow combine practicality with prettiness. The Oxford pillowcases are easy to make and can be made from whatever material you have in your fabric stash. The laundry bag is big enough for a couple to use and can be taken away with them, if they want, and the candle bag, below, is just a lovely welcome gift.

A *Pretty* Candle Bag

YOU WILL NEED:

- Fabric (50cm x 50cm)
- Measuring tape
- Scissors
- Pins
- Sewing cotton
- Sewing machine
- Pencil and compass
- Ribbon
  (70cm (l) x 1 cm (w)
- Candle

NOTE: This is based on a candle measuring 9cm x 7.5cm. Please adjust accordingly.

TO MAKE THE OUTSIDE OF THE BAG

1. From the fabric cut a piece measuring 26cm x 26cm. Pin and sew a double hem (5mm per fold) along the top edge of the fabric (*see image 1, right*).

2. Lay the fabric face down in front of you, with the hemmed edge facing right. Fold the fabric in half towards you and pin the long bottom edge together. Sew 5mm in from the edge to create an open-ended tube.

TO MAKE THE BASE

3. Use the leftover fabric to make the candle bag base. Use the pencil and compass to draw a circle with a 10cm-diameter onto the back of the fabric and cut this out. Turn the material pattern-side up and pin the base to the unhemmed end of the open-ended tube, 1cm in from the outer edge of the circle. Sew the base to the tube, sticking as close to the border allowance as possible to avoid ruffling the fabric (*see image 2, right*).

4. Trim 5mm of the excess material from the circular base so that it lies flat. This will enable the candle to sit inside properly. Turn the bag the right way out (*see image 3, right*).

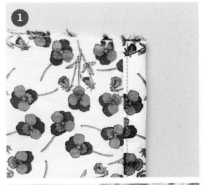

TO DECORATE THE CANDLE BAG

5. From the top edge, measure down the joining seam 7cm. Take the ribbon and secure it in place with several 1mm-wide stitches (*see image 4*).

TO TIE THE BAG

6. Place the candle inside the bag. Take the ends of the ribbon and wrap them around the top of the bag so that they meet at the front. Tie the ribbon in a bow (*see photo, above*).

A *Pair* of Oxford Pillowcases

MAKES: 2 (80cm x 53cm)

YOU WILL NEED:

- Fabric (2m x 1.10m)
- Measuring tape
- Scissors (paper/fabric)
- Pins
- Sewing cotton
- Sewing machine
- Iron and ironing board

NOTE: I suggest using quilting fabric, brushed cotton or Egyptian cotton.

TO MAKE THE PILLOWCASES

1. From the fabric, cut a piece measuring 195cm (l) x 55cm (w). Pin and sew a double hem (1.5cm per hem) at both ends of the 55cm edge.

2. Lay the fabric out flat, pattern-side up. Fold 1 of the hemmed ends over and in on itself by 74cm (*see image 1*). Fold the other end of the fabric over by exactly 35cm so that it lies over the first fold (*see image 2*). There should be a gap of 5cm between where the folded piece of fabric ends and the top edge of the pillow starts.

3. Pin the 2 open side edges of the pillowcase 1cm from the edge, making sure all the layers are secured together. Sew into place. Turn the pillowcase the right way out and iron flat (*see image 3*).

4. To create the border, measure 4cm in from the outside edge on all 4 sides. Sew in place, using a 2mm-running stitch (*see image 4*). Repeat the above steps to make the second pillowcase from the remaining fabric.

Giant Laundry Bag

TO MAKE THE LOWER AND TOP SECTIONS

1. Take the fabric for the lower section and cut a piece measuring 110cm (l) x 54cm (w). Pin and sew a double hem (1cm per fold) along the 2 x 54cm edges and set to one side (*see image 1, right*).

2. Then from the top section fabric, cut and measure 2 pieces of fabric, each measuring 56cm (l) x 29cm (w). Take 1 of the pieces and pin a double hem (1cm per hem) along the 2 x 29cm sides and along the bottom edge of the fabric. Sew the hems in place, removing the pins as you go.

3. Fold the unhemmed top edge over by 1cm and then fold it over again a further 6cm. Pin in place 6cm down along the folded edge. Sew 3mm up from the bottom all the way along (*see image 2, right*).

4. Measure 3cm down from the top edge of the fabric and sew all the way across the width of the fabric, doing this creates 2 channels of stitches for the cord to be threaded through. Do not sew the sides wclosed.

5. Repeat these steps with the remaining piece of fabric for the top section. You will end up with 2 identical pieces of fabric (*see image 3, right*).

YOU WILL NEED

- Fabric for lower section (150cm x 100cm)
- Fabric for top section (100cm x 100cm)
- Measuring tape
- Scissors
- Pins
- Sewing cotton
- Sewing machine
- 2m cord
- Sewing needle
- Iron and ironing board

TIP

To embroider the word 'Laundry', write the word out in fabric pen on the front top section of the bag and embroider over it using a chain or running stitch with embroidery thread.

TO SEW THE BAG TOGETHER

6. Lay the lower section of the bag face up on a flat surface. Take 1 top section piece and lay it face down (with the 2 channels at the bottom) so the edges meet up. Pin in place. Sew both sections together 2cm in from the pinned edge, just underneath the hem. Iron the seams out flat. Repeat the process with the second top piece of fabric (*see image 4*).

7. Fold the bag in half inwards, making sure that the sides and top edge of the bag line up. Pin and sew together the sides of the lower section 5mm in from the edge. Turn the bag the right way out (*see image 5*).

8. To strengthen the bag, sew a 1cm border around the sides and bottom edges of the lower section. Thread the cord through the lower channel on either side of the bag in the top section.

9. To prevent the ends of the cord from unravelling, cut out 4 pieces of fabric, each measuring 4cm x 4cm. Pin 2 of the pieces together, face to face, around the end of the cord so that the fabric encases the cord. Trim off the top corners and sew along the sides and along the top. This leaves the bottom edge open. Handstitch the fabric to the cord (*see image 6*).

10. Turn the fabric the right way out and sew closed what is now the top edge of the cord covering.

It's late on Sunday morning in my kitchen and I've opted to make the mother of all roasts, a roast rib of beef (rare) with all the trimmings, including my famous gravy and crispy roast potatoes.

A Rib of Beef

SERVES: 4

INGREDIENTS
4kg rib of beef
400g carrots, trimmed
300g leeks, cut lengthways
200g celery, trimmed
250g shallots, unpeeled
30g plain flour, sifted
½ tsp sea salt
½ tsp black pepper
15g fresh rosemary

SPECIAL EQUIPMENT
Meat thermometer

MEAT TEMPERATURE GUIDE	
Rare:	60°C
Medium:	71°C
Well done:	82°C

Preheat the oven to 240°C/Gas 9. If chilled, leave the meat to rest until it reaches room temperature.

Put all the vegetables close to one another in a large roasting tin. They will act as a 'trivet' for the meat and also add flavour to the gravy later. Sprinkle flour, salt and pepper onto the sides and top of the joint and place it upright on top of the vegetables.

Place on the middle shelf of the preheated oven and roast for 20 minutes. Take the meat out of the oven and reduce the oven temperature to 160°C/Gas 3. Push sprigs of rosemary beneath the joint of meat and put it back in the oven. Cook for a further 1 hour 40 minutes if you want rare meat; 2 hours 25 minutes for medium meat and 2 hours, 50 minutes for well-done meat.

As the meat is cooking, baste it regularly (but quickly) in the juices and use the meat thermometer to test its temperature from the thickest part of the joint. Don't rely on the timings alone. When the meat has reached its required temperature – in this case 60°C – take it out of the oven. Lift the joint out of the roasting tin, but leave the vegetables there to use to make the gravy (*see opposite*).

Place the meat on a wooden board and leave it to rest at room temperature for 1 hour. Depending on how well the meat is cooked, juice may seep out onto the board. If you can, add the juice to the gravy; if not, have some kitchen paper to hand to absorb it.

...*with* Beef Gravy

SERVES: 4

INGREDIENTS
Vegetables from rib of beef
500ml red wine
1 tbsp Worcestershire sauce
1 tsp Marmite
2 tbsp plain flour
400ml boiling water
1 star anise

Remove the vegetables and cooking juices from the roasting tin and cook them, over a medium heat, in a large pan. Be careful not to let any burnt bits from the tray go into the pan, as this will make the gravy taste bitter.

Pour in the wine, then add the Worcestershire sauce, Marmite, 1 tablespoon of the flour and half the boiling water and stir for 5 minutes. Strain the pan contents through a sieve. Discard the vegetables and pour the gravy back into the pan; add the star anise and return to a low heat. Pour in the rest of the boiling water and flour, stirring until any lumps disappear. Heat gently for a further 10 minutes, stirring regularly.

Serving suggestion: Serve in a warmed gravy boat.

Horseradish Sauce

There's no greater marriage than beef with freshly made horseradish sauce. Mmm ...

MAKES: 150g

INGREDIENTS
80g fresh horseradish,
    grated
100ml crème fraîche
3–4 tsp cider vinegar
¼ tsp caster sugar
Salt

Put the grated horseradish in a medium-sized bowl.

Stir in the crème fraîche, vinegar, sugar and the salt to taste.
Mix together well with a spoon.

Cover the bowl with cling film and put in the fridge until ready
to serve. This can be made the day before to save time.

TIP   If kept in the fridge in a sterilised and sealed jam jar, the horseradish sauce will keep
for up to one week.

Traditional Yorkshire Puddings

SERVES: 4

INGREDIENTS
125g plain flour
2 large eggs
140ml full-fat milk
Salt
3 tbsp vegetable oil

SPECIAL EQUIPMENT
12-hole cupcake tin
(holes; 7.5cm x 3.5cm)

Preheat the oven to 220°C/Gas 7. Sift the flour into a large bowl. Make a well in the middle; add 1 egg and 110ml of milk. Use a balloon whisk to mix together until smooth. Remove any lumps.

Add the second egg and the rest of the milk and continue to whisk the mixture together until the batter is lump-free and the consistency is rather runny.

Grease the holes of the cupcake tin with oil and put it in the preheated oven for 3–4 minutes, until the oil is very hot. The batter needs to sizzle as it hits the oil.

Divide the batter evenly between the holes in the tin; they should be half-full. Put in the oven and cook for 10 minutes, then turn the temperature down to 180°C/Gas 4 for 5 minutes, or until the puddings are golden and crispy. These quantities can also be used to make 1 large pudding.

Crispy Roast Potatoes

SERVES: 4

INGREDIENTS
2.5kg Maris Piper potatoes,
   cut into quarters
340g tin goose fat
5 large garlic cloves
Salt
Ground black pepper

Preheat the oven to 220°C/Gas 7.

In a large pan, over a medium heat, bring salted water to the boil. Add the potato quarters and boil for 5 minutes. Put the goose fat and the unpeeled garlic cloves in a large roasting tin and place in the preheated oven for 8–10 minutes, or until the fat is extremely hot.

Drain the potatoes and put them back into the saucepan, this time cook over a very low heat. Shake the pan back and forth so that the pototoes bash gently against the sides. This helps remove any remaining moisture and makes them extra fluffy for roasting.

Remove the roasting tin from the oven and carefully place the potatoes in the hot goose fat and garlic. Season with salt and pepper to taste before putting it back in the oven. Roast for 1 hour, or until golden and crunchy.

... *and* Parmesan Roast Parsnips

SERVES: 4

INGREDIENTS
750g parsnips, cut in half
   lengthways
4 tbsp groundnut oil
75g plain flour
50g Parmesan cheese, grated
Salt
Ground black pepper

Preheat the oven to 220°C/Gas 7.

In a large pan, over a medium heat, bring water to to the boil. Add the parsnips and boil for 5 minutes. Remove from the heat, but do not drain.

Pour the oil into a large roasting tin and place in the preheated oven. In a large bowl, mix together the flour, Parmesan, salt and pepper. Drain the parsnips and while they are still hot, coat them in the flour–Parmesan mix.

Remove the roasting tin from the oven and use tongs to carefully place the parsnips in the tin. Put in the oven and roast for about 30 minutes, or until crunchy. Turn them a few times to help the parsnips cook evenly.

Steamed Ginger and Treacle Pudding

We Brits are famous for our steamed puds and there's nothing quite like a piping hot ginger and treacle pudding on a wintry day to end a Sunday lunch with friends.

SERVES: 4

INGREDIENTS
2 tbsp golden syrup
115g unsalted butter,
   softened, plus extra
   for greasing
115g caster sugar
115g self-raising flour
1 tsp ground ginger
2 large eggs

SPECIAL EQUIPMENT
500ml pudding basin;
about 3m string

Pour the syrup into the pudding basin and grease the rest of the inside of the basin with butter above the top of the syrup.

In the bowl of a free-standing mixer, use the paddle attachment to cream the butter and sugar until light and fluffy. Sift in the flour and ginger, then add the eggs and blend until smooth and glossy.

Pour the batter on top of the syrup and cover the top of the basin with greaseproof paper. Secure the paper in place using half the string. Wrap it around the top of the basin, just underneath the rim, and tie with a knot. Cover the top of the greaseproof paper with tin foil and use the remaining string to secure that in place, as before.

Put the pudding basin in a large pan of boiling water over a low heat; the water level should sit just below the top edge of the pudding basin.

Let the water simmer, thus allowing the pudding to be steamed. Check the water periodically and, if necessary, top it up.

After 1½ hours, remove the basin from the boiling water and leave it to cool for at least 20 minutes.

Remove the tin foil and the greaseproof paper from the basin and carefully turn the bowl upside down onto a serving dish. Carefully remove the pudding from the basin.

Serving suggestion: Lovely served warm with good-quality vanilla ice cream or custard.

Christmas

I TEND TO GO A LITTLE CRAZY AT CHRISTMAS TIME. I'm a self-confessed lover of anything to do with this time of year. I love the preparation, which starts, for me, in late summer, when I pick up gifts at the sales. I love the music and food, of course, but most of all, I love the change of atmosphere in my home, the warmth and cosiness of it all.

I was raised in a home in which Christmas was special. It was an absolutely sacred time for us, full of peace and happiness and I have my parents to thank for that. I remember clearly that my siblings and I were never naughty at Christmas or, at least, we were never told off.

As a young adult living in London, I made muffins for the Christmas delivery drivers and decorated my front door with a homemade wreath (*see pages 244–47*). My flat was so small that I had a tiny tree and my poor cat ended up more decorated than the rest of the place! Luckily, I married a man who loves Christmas as much as I do and, now that we have children, I'm trying to brainwash them into our way of thinking.

I could fill a million books with ideas for Christmas but, as I only have one chapter, I am going to concentrate on how to entertain your Christmas visitors; whether it be a neighbour who's popped across the road with a card, your child's play dates and their parents or friends and workmates, invited over for some mince pies and tree biscuits.

Whatever the occasion, this chapter includes some lovely things to either feed to your guests or to present to them as gifts. So … *welcome to my Christmas Wonderland*!

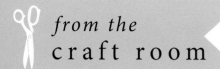

the

craft room

A Gingerbread Village

There's nothing like the smell of gingerbread to summon up Christmas, but why not go one step further and make a gingerbread house or, if you're like me and love all things Christmas, something a bit more ambitious … a gingerbread village. I know that this sounds like a huge amount of work, but it's surprising what can be achieved in a relatively small amount of time. Simply set the village up on a table, covered with a snowy white cloth and draped in fairy lights, candles and the odd reindeer and you will be astonished at how lovely it looks. It's also a really great place to display foodie gifts, such as the mince pies and tree biscuits found later in the chapter. The following spreads (*pages 230–35*) give instructions, in 3 easy stages, on how to make and assemble the gingerbread village:

STAGE 1 provides templates for the 3 gingerbread houses.

STAGE 2 shows you how to make the all important gingerbread.

STAGE 3 provides instructions on how to assemble and decorate the houses.

STEP by STEP

Making Gingerbread Houses in 3 *Easy* Stages

 STAGE 1 TO MAKE THE TEMPLATES FOR THE HOUSES

The following 4 pages (*pages 230–33*) are dedicated to Stage 1 of the process, making the templates. While you can, of course, make the houses at whatever size you want, the ones in my village come in 3 sizes: small, medium and large.

Below you will find the dimensions for the front/back; roof and sides of each house. On pages 231–33, I have also provided templates (drawn at 100 per cent) for each house.

THE DIMENSIONS OF THE HOUSES:

• SMALL HOUSE

Front/Back:
5cm (h) x 8cm (w)

Roof x 2:
4.8cm (h) x 8cm (w)

Side x 2:
9cm (h) x 5cm (w);
5cm (*angled roof support*)

• MEDIUM HOUSE

Front/Back:
9cm (h) x 11cm (w)

Roof x 2:
8cm (h) x 11cm (w)

Side x 2:
15cm (h) x 11cm (w);
9cm (*angled roof support*)

• LARGE HOUSE

Front/Back:
15cm (h) x 21cm (w)

Roof x 2:
9.5cm (h) x 21cm (w)

Side x 2:
21cm (h) x 15cm (w);
15cm (*angled roof support*)

YOU WILL NEED:
- 9 x A4 sheets tracing paper
- Pencil
- Scissors

To make the templates simply place a sheet of tracing paper over these pages and draw around the outlines. Each template can be used twice.

Use scissors to cut the templates out carefully and put to one side while you go to Stage 2.

FRONT/BACK X 2
TEMPLATE

small

medium

large

ROOF X 2
TEMPLATE

small

medium

large

SIDE X 2
TEMPLATE

small

medium

large

STAGE 2 TO MAKE THE GINGERBREAD

MAKES: 3 houses
(small, medium and large)

INGREDIENTS
Gingerbread
300g light brown
    muscovado sugar
200g margarine, softened
250g black treacle
1.1kg plain flour, plus extra
    for dusting
2 tsp bicarbonate of soda
1 tsp salt
¼ tsp ground cloves
1 tsp ground cinnamon
2 tsp ground ginger
250ml water

Icing mortar
1kg icing sugar
2 tsp cream of tartar
6 large egg whites

SPECIAL EQUIPMENT
Baking tray (38cm x 30cm);
parchment paper; piping
bag with a small nozzle
attachment; wire rack;
cake boards/stands

Preheat the oven to 220°C/Gas 7. Line the baking tray with the parchment paper. You will need to bake the gingerbread in batches.

In a free-standing mixer, use a paddle attachment to cream the sugar and margarine. Add the black treacle and mix until a smooth paste forms.

In a large bowl, mix together the flour, bicarbonate of soda, salt, cloves, cinnamon and ginger. Gradually add the sugar–treacle paste and water, stirring well, until it becomes the consistency of bread dough – thick, strong and slightly stretchy. It is ready when it can be removed from the bowl without it sticking.

On a well-floured surface, roll out the gingerbread dough to a thickness of 3–4mm. Lay the paper templates on top of the dough and use a very sharp knife to cut out the 2 side walls, 2 end walls and 2 roof pieces per house.

Place the pieces on the prepared lined baking tray and put in the preheated oven. Bake for 10–12 minutes, before removing and allowing to cool on a wire rack.

To make the icing mortar, in the clean bowl of the mixer, use the whisk attachment to mix together the sifted icing sugar, cream of tartar and egg whites until it thickens. It is ready when it forms stiff peaks.

Spoon the icing into a piping bag with a small nozzle attachment.

TIP   Use a cutter to create gingerbread biscuits or men. Place 4 or 5 in a pretty gift box, lined with coloured tissue paper. This makes the perfect present for your guests!

TO ASSEMBLE AND DECORATE YOUR VILLAGE

Decoration

Frosted wheats for the roof tiles

Selection of sweets – such as jelly babies, liquorice allsorts, candy canes, jelly tots, pink and white chocolate buttons, smarties

TO ASSEMBLE THE HOUSES

1. Take 3 cake boards/stands and place on a clean flat surface.

2. To assemble, start with the large house. Take the back and front walls and generously pipe the icing mortar along the side and top edges. Do the same with the side walls, but leave the roof for now.

3. Carefully push the 4 walls together and hold in place (you may need an extra pair of hands or, alternatively, use a box or a jar to prop the walls up from the inside). If necessary, add more mortar. Leave to dry for at least 30 minutes, or for as long as possible.

4. Take the roof pieces and generously pipe the mortar along the edges. Carefully place the roof panels on top of the 4 walls. This can be tricky as the angle is steep. Again, you may need an extra pair of hands to hold it in place for at least a minute, while it begins to set. The longer it is held the stronger it will be.

5. Repeat this process with the other 2 houses. Leave to dry. Cover the remaining icing mortar with cling film for use when decorating.

TO DECORATE THE HOUSES

6. Fill a piping bag with the remaining icing and pipe swirls onto the roof. Take some frosted wheats and press into place. Pipe small dots onto the gingerbread houses. Use to stick sweets of your choice in place.

7. Clean around the cake board/stands and leave the houses to dry. Then create your village.

At Christmas time, the kitchen takes some beating. I plan my festive food from mid- to late October and then on the last Sunday before Advent I hold Stir-up Sunday in my kitchen. My friends – both male and female I hasten to add – and I gather with our clean jars and pudding basins and make Christmas pudding, Christmas cake and mincemeat. I have included the following recipes, however, because they are easy and quick to make. Most can be prepared a day or so in advance and kept on hand for those unexpected visitors, who always seem to drop by. Also, by simply placing a few cakes or peppermint creams in a pretty box, tissue paper or cellophane, with a pretty ribbon wrapped around, they become a perfect gift for guests.

Super-fast Mince Pies

MAKES: 18–24

INGREDIENTS
Mince pies
Plain flour for dusting
2 x 500g block sweetened
  shortcrust pastry
820g jar mincemeat

Buttercream
150g unsalted butter, softened,
1 tsp vanilla extract
300g icing sugar, sifted

SPECIAL EQUIPMENT
12-hole cupcake tin; 7cm-round cookie cutter; 5cm-star cookie cutter; piping bag with a large nozzle attachment

Preheat the oven to 200°C/Gas 6. Grease the 12-hole cupcake tin and the baking tray. Sprinkle a little flour onto a surface and roll out the pastry to a thickness of 1cm.

Use the round cookie cutter to cut out the pastry into 18–24 rounds. Press into the cupcake tin moulds. Place a teaspoon of mincemeat into each pastry case.

Roll out the leftover pastry and cut out the lids with the star shaped cutter. Lay them out on a baking tray. Place the pastry cases and stars in the preheated oven and bake for 15 minutes (or until a light golden brown). Remove from oven; leave to cool for 15 minutes as mincemeat will be hot.

To make the buttercream, in the bowl of a free-standing mixer, use the paddle attachment to cream together the butter, vanilla extract and icing sugar until white and fluffy. Fill the piping bag (with a large nozzle attachment) and pipe a generous swirl with the buttercream onto each cooled pie. To finish, top with a pastry star and dust with icing sugar.

Chocolate and Ice Cupcakes

MAKES: 12

INGREDIENTS

Cupcakes
170g caster sugar
170g unsalted butter, room
  temperature
3 large eggs, beaten
170g self-raising flour, sifted
2 heaped tbsp of cocoa
  powder
1 tsp black food colouring

Buttercream
150g unsalted butter, softened,
  plus extra for greasing
1 tsp vanilla extract
300g icing sugar, sifted
A few drops of baby blue food
  colouring

Optional
80g jar edible silver pearls

SPECIAL EQUIPMENT
12-hole cupcake tin; cupcake
cases; piping bag with a
large nozzle attachment

Preheat the oven to 180°C/Gas 4. Fill the 12-hole cupcake tin with cupcake cases.

In the bowl of a free-standing mixer, use the paddle attachment to beat the sugar and butter together until light in colour and fluffy. Continue beating while gradually adding the eggs; to prevent curdling at this point add in a little flour. Gently fold in the flour, cocoa and food colouring and mix until smooth.

Spoon the batter into the cases until just over half-full. Put the tin in the preheated oven and bake for 15–20 minutes, or until the sponge bounces back when touched. A skewer inserted into a cake should come out clean. Remove from the oven and allow to cool.

To make the buttercream, in the clean bowl of the mixer blend together the butter, vanilla extract, icing sugar until fluffy. Add in a few drops of food colouring and mix until an even colour. Then spoon the buttercream into a piping bag with a large nozzle attachment.

Start piping a spiral of buttercream from the outside edge of the cupcake and work inwards and upwards. Finish off with a flourish!

I like to decorate my cakes with edible silver balls (or pearls) – but watch your teeth on those pesky things!

TIP These cakes can be made the night before and stored in a Tupperware container, with layers of greaseproof paper between the cakes. Decorate with the buttercream on the day of use.

Cherry's Pud Pot Gifts

MAKES: 4

INGREDIENTS
450g Christmas pudding

Brandy Butter
170g unsalted butter,
4 tbsp brandy
1 tsp almond extract
170g icing sugar, sifted

Decoration
24 hazelnuts
12 squares dark chocolate

SPECIAL EQUIPMENT
4 x 450ml mason jars;
piping bag with a large
nozzle attachment

Cook the Christmas pudding according to the instructions. Divide evenly between the 4 x 450ml clean mason jars.

To make the brandy butter, in the bowl of a free-standing mixer, use a paddle attachment to blend the butter, brandy and almond extract. Add the icing sugar to the mixture and whip until smooth and pale. Spoon the brandy butter into the piping bag with a large nozzle attachment; pipe the brandy butter onto the top of each pudding, swirling round and working inwards and upwards so that it finishes in a peak. Make sure the butter is not higher than the jar rim.

In a frying pan, over a medium heat, dry fry the hazelnuts for about 3–4 minutes, shaking them to make sure they do not burn. Allow them to cool before wrapping them in a tea towel to rub off the skins. Roughly chop the nuts and the chocolate squares. Sprinkle generously onto the brandy butter.

Serving suggestion: Screw the lid on and tie a spoon on with ribbon.

Peppermint Creams

MAKES: 12

INGREDIENTS
2 large egg whites
Juice of 1 lemon
2 tsp peppermint flavouring
800g icing sugar, sifted,
   plus extra for dusting
A few drops of food
   colouring

SPECIAL EQUIPMENT
5cm-round cookie cutter

In the clean bowl of a free-standing mixer, use a whisk attachment to beat the egg whites until they form stiff peaks.

Change the whisk to the paddle attachment. While the machine is on, and the paddle is turning, slowly add the lemon juice, peppermint flavouring and icing sugar (and any food colouring) and mix until it forms a stiff paste.

Tip the paste onto a surface lightly dusted with icing sugar and roll out to a thickness of 4mm. Use the round cookie cutter to cut out the peppermint creams; lay them out on a baking tray and chill for 1–2 hours, or until firm.

Christmas Tree Biscuits

This easy recipe is very versatile. Use a Christmas tree-shaped cookie cutter to make the biscuits festive and stand the finished pieces up in your Winter Wonderland to make an edible forest. Box some up to make gifts. Or, for a really festive treat, serve with hot chocolate, with a glug of Baileys topped with some squirty cream and marshmallows. Delicious!

MAKES: 18

INGREDIENTS
Tree biscuits
200g of unsalted butter, softened
200g of caster sugar
1 large egg, beaten
400g plain flour, sifted, plus extra for dusting

Decoration
250g pack Regal-Ice ready-to-roll icing
45g jar edible sugar balls

SPECIAL EQUIPMENT
Parchment paper;
Tree-shaped cookie cutter

Preheat the oven to 180°C/Gas 4. Line a baking sheet with the parchment paper.

In the bowl of a free-standing mixer, use the paddle attachment to cream the butter and sugar together until just combined. Beat the egg into the mixture; add the flour and mix in until it all comes together to form a soft dough ball. It is ready when the dough comes away from the side of the bowl. Wrap in cling film and chill for 30 minutes, or until cold.

Sprinkle a surface with flour and roll out the dough to a thickness of 5mm. Use the tree-shaped cookie cutter to cut out the biscuits. Place the biscuits, well spaced out, on the lined baking sheet. Chill again for 30 minutes. Place in the preheated oven for 6–8 minutes, or until the biscuits are cream in colour (I don't even allow them to turn golden). Remove from the oven.

While still warm, roll out the icing to a thickness of about 5mm. Use the tree-shaped cookie cutter to cut out the icing. Place each shape on a biscuit, pressing the icing down into place lightly but firmly. Finish with a few decorative sugar balls.

TIP If the cookies aren't warm, dab some water onto the back of the icing before placing onto the cookie. Press down firmly.

A Simply *Lovely* Christmas Wreath

The garden is deep in hibernation at this time of year but that doesn't mean there aren't some fantastic pieces of foliage to rescue for a homemade wreath. Make friends with some very thin florist wire and you'll be twisting your way to a fabulous decoration for your front door. Or, simply lay it flat on the table and put a candle in the middle for a great table decoration.

YOU WILL NEED:

Christmas greenery
(eucalyptis, conifer, ivy,
mistletoe)
Oasis foam ring/natural twig
wreath (about 40cm
diameter)
4m florist wire
Berries (such as holly
berries, snowberries)
Dried fruit (such as
pomegranate, ruby
grapefruit, bramley apples)
2m ribbon (such as silk
or velvet)
2m string

NOTE: For instructions and tips on how to dry fruit, see page 247; for instructions on how to tie a classic bow, see page 197.

TO MAKE YOUR SIMPLE HOMEMADE WREATH

- Gather any Christmassy greenery from the garden – eucalyptus, conifer, ivy and mistletoe are great for this purpose. Take a ready-made wreath of your choice, such as an Oasis foam ring or a natural twig wreath (available from local garden centres) and cover it by pushing the foliage into the pre-soaked foam or through the twigs.

- Use florist wire to twist around holly berries, snowberries, dried pomegranates, dried slices of ruby grapefruit and even large dried slices of bramley apples. A truly beautiful wreath is bursting with fruit, foliage and colour so, in this case, 'less' really isn't 'more'.

- Attach the fruits to the foliage-decorated wreath. Adorn it with a red or deep pink bow. Then, all you have to do is attach it to your doorknocker or nail – and voilà, in less than an hour, you have assembled a wreath that looks like it has come straight from a professional florist.

TIP
My Christmas wreaths drip with roses. Coupled with the pale green eucalyptus, creamy white of snowberries, the cool vibrancy of blousy pink roses is a festive marriage made in heaven. They also last surprisingly well on the door!

Drying *tips*

Why buy expensive dried fruit when you can dry your own at home? Simply lovely on a wreath or as part of a table setting, here are some tips on how to dry the fruit I love most.

WHOLE POMEGRANATES

- Start 2–3 weeks before you need them. Cut 6 very small slits, about 1cm in length and depth into the skin of the pomegranate.

- Place the pomegranate onto a wire rack; air needs to circulate around it. Place the rack on top of the boiler, the right-hand side of the top of an Aga cooker if you have one, or any other warm dry place in your home.

- Leave to dry until they go hard. Not every drop of the juice inside will be eliminated, but the fruit will be dry enough to hang on your wreath or use as a table decoration.

SLICES OF RUBY RED GRAPEFRUITS OR ORANGES

- Start a week before you need the fruit. Slice the grapefruit or orange into 1cm thick slices. Blot the slices dry with kitchen roll. You won't soak up all the juice, but you'll certainly be able to get them started.

- Put the slices on a wire rack and place it in a warm dry place. If the slices are very juicy, then place a plate underneath the rack to catch any drips.

- Another way to dry fruit is place the rack underneath a warm/hot radiator. Or, lay sheets of kitchen roll across the top of a radiator and place your slices along it.

Other *uses*

- **TABLE DECORATION:** Follow the instructions for the wreath on page 244. Place it face up on the table with a single fat church candle in the middle. Fill in any gaps with extra foliage.

- **TREE DECORATIONS:** Simply thread the fruit onto pretty ribbon or bakers' twine. Hang from your tree or from branches collected from the garden or park.

- **GIFT TAGS:** Attach a piece of hessian or twine to a slice of pink grapefruit along with a traditional parcel tag (*see page 143 for label template*). Tie to present.

Conversion Charts

WEIGHT CONVERSIONS
Grams to Ounces

Metric	Imperial
7g	¼oz
15g	½oz
20g	¾oz
25g	1oz
40g	1½oz
50g	2oz
60g	2½oz
100g	3½oz
125g	4oz
140g	4½oz
150g	5oz
165g	5½oz
175g	6oz
200g	7oz
225g	8oz
250g	9oz
275g	10oz
300g	11oz
350g	12oz
375g	13oz
400g	14oz
425g	15oz
450g	1lb
500g	1lb 2oz
550g	1¼lb
600g	1lb 5oz
650g	1lb 7oz
675g	1½lb
700g	1lb 9oz
750g	1lb 11oz
800g	1¾lb
900g	2lb
1kg	2¼lb
1.1kg	2½lb
1.25kg	2¾lb
1.35kg	3lb
1.5kg	3lb 6oz
1.8kg	4lb
2kg	4½lb
2.25kg	5lb
2.5kg	5½lb
2.75kg	6lb

OVEN TEMPERATURE CONVERSIONS

Fahrenheit	Celsius	Gas Mark	Heat of Oven
225	110	¼	Very cool
250	120	½	Very cool
275	140	1	Cool
300	150	2	Cool
325	160	3	Moderate
350	180	4	Moderate
375	190	5	Moderately hot
400	200	6	Moderately hot
425	220	7	Hot
450	230	8	Hot
475	240	9	Very hot

VOLUME CONVERSIONS
Millilitres to Fluid Ounces and US Cups

Metric	Imperial	US Cups
25ml	1fl oz	
50ml	2fl oz	¼ cup
75ml	3fl oz	
100ml	3½fl oz	
120ml	4fl oz	½ cup
150ml	5fl oz	
175ml	6fl oz	¾ cup
200ml	7fl oz	
250ml	8fl oz	1 cup
300ml	10fl oz/½ pint	1¼ cup
360ml	12fl oz	
400ml	14fl oz	
450ml	15fl oz	2 cups
600ml	1 pint	2 ½ cups
750ml	1¼ pints	
900ml	1½ pints	
1 litre	1¾ pints	1 quart
1.2 litres	2 pints	
1.4 litres	2½ pints	
1.5 litres	2¾ pints	
1.7 litres	3 pints	
2 litres	3½ pints	
3 litres	5¼ pints	

Kitchen: Store Cupboard Essentials

BAKING/KITCHEN EQUIPMENT

If you have some basic tools and equipment in your kitchen not only will they stand you in very good stead, but your confidence will also soar.

GENERAL

- Balloon whisk
- Chopping board: I use a wooden chopping board and four different plastic chopping boards, specifically the Joseph 'Index' set.
- Cast-iron casserole/Dutch oven
- Knife: My 18cm-general purpose Santoku 'three uses' knife is used frequently in my kitchen.
- Large mixing bowl
- Non-stick frying pan with a lid, 26cm
- Parchment paper
- Rolling pin: I use three on a regular basis, a long chunky wooden rolling pin with handles; a slender, round-ended wooden rolling pin for smaller quantities of food and pastry; and a 23cm-plastic rolling pin for sugar craft and fine baking.
- Sieve
- Silicon spatula
- Tongs
- Wooden spoon: I have four or five in various lengths.

COOKING/BAKING

- Cookie cutters: Various shapes such as Christmas tree, gingerbread, person, heart, egg, star, square, round
- Cooking thermometer
- Measuring cups: I do a lot of cooking and baking involving American quantities, so being able to transfer cup measurements into millilitres or into grams is essential.
- Measuring jug: A Pyrex 0.5 litre jug

- Measuring spoons
- Meat thermometer: Used to measure the internal temperature of meat and therefore determining how the meat is cooked.
- Mezzaluna: My preferred way of chopping herbs quickly and finely.
- Pie weights/Baking beans: Usually ceramic
- Piping bag and nozzle(s)
- Weighing scales
- Hand-held zester

BAKING TRAYS

- Non-stick baking tray: I use two 38cm x 30cm trays to bake cookies, biscuits, pizza and even fish on.
- Roasting tin
- Trivet: I have a metal trivet right next to my oven hob to protect tabletops and work surfaces from heat damage.

CAKE/TART/FLAN TINS

- 12-hole bun tins: Tin with a 3cm-deep hole is a general-purpose tin.
- Ceramic tart/flan dish: A 26cm-dish will accommodate most tart recipes.
- Loose-bottom cake tin: I am a huge fan of loose-bottomed cake tins; they create a cake with a neater finish and there is less risk of them breaking.
- Small tartlet tins: Generally non-stick with a loose bottom, a 10-cm diameter is a good size tin. Keep 4–6 in the kitchen cupboard.

STAPLE FOOD CUPBOARD INGREDIENTS

I've listed a few of my favourite brands below which are usually easy to find in a large range of supermarkets.

- **Eggs:** All the recipes use large, free-range eggs
- **Butter:** All the recipes use unsalted butter

BAKING GOODS
Baking powder, bicarbonate of soda (baking soda), cocoa powder, cream of tartar, fast-action yeast, gelatin leaves, almond and vanilla extract (I use Neilsen Massey)

TINS AND JARS
Capers, chick peas, kidney beans, olives (pitted, black and green), tomatoes (chopped)

CONDIMENTS
Aioli mayonnaise, French's American mustard, Dijon mustard, Heinz tomato ketchup, Hellman's mayonnaise, Kikkoman Soy sauce and Tabasco Sauce, Lea & Perrins Worcestershire sauce

DECORATION
Edible silver balls, fondant icing, food colouring or paste (I like Squires Kitchen), icing sugar, liquid glucose, royal icing

FLOUR AND PASTRY
- **Flour:** Bread, corn, plain, self-raising, strong, wholemeal, gluten-free (Doves Farm)
- **Pastry:** Readymade puff, readymade short crust, readymade dessert

GRAINS
Couscous, popping corn, pasta (assorted shapes), quinoa, rice (arborio, basmati, brown)

HERBS AND SPICES
- **Dried:** Basil, bay, coriander and fennel seeds, marjoram, mixed herbs, oregano, parsley, rosemary, sage, tarragon, thyme
- **Fresh:** Basil, bay leaves, coriander, chives, dill, lemon thyme, mint, oregano, parsley, rosemary, sage, tarragon, thyme
- **Ground:** Allspice, black pepper, chilli powder, cinnamon, cloves, cumin, ginger, nutmeg, paprika, white pepper

OILS AND VINEGARS
Balsamic reduction, balsamic vinegar, chilli oil, extra virgin olive oil, groundnut oil, red wine vinegar, sunflower, toasted sesame oil, white wine vinegar

SUGARS
Caster, demerara, granulated, muscovado (light and dark), vanilla

SYRUPS
Chocolate, maple, rose, strawberry (I use the Monin syrups)

Craft Essentials

EQUIPMENT

Card and paper (assorted sizes), A4 paper, A4 tracing paper; **Cutting mat** (60cm x 45cm is a good size); **Craft glue**; **Craft wire**; **Decorative stickers and embellishments**; **Embroidery hoops**; **Needles** (sewing and embroidery); **Paint brushes** (various sizes); **Pencil/pen**; **Pins** (sewing, drawing); **Pin cushion**; **Ruler**; **Scissors** (paper/pinking/fabric); **Sticky tape**

INSTRUMENTS

Drawing compass; **Hot glue gun**; **Iron/ironing board**; **Measuring tape**; **Rotary cutter/rotary ruler**; **Seam unpicker**; **Sewing machine**

TEXTILES

Bias binding; **Buttons** (assorted sizes); **Cord**; **Embroidery thread**; **Fabric scraps**; **Felt** (various colours, sizes, thicknesses); **Ribbon** (cotton, grosgrain, ric-rac, satin, velvet, wire-edged); **Sewing cotton** (selection of colours); **Stash of various fabrics** (quilting, household, upholstery); **String**; **Stuffing** (polyester); **Wadding** (bamboo, cotton); **Wool**; **Yarn**

TIP If you have any scraps of fabric left over from projects, no matter how large or small, save them all in a basket. These scraps will come in useful either for stuffing cushions, toys, and so on, or for making patchwork pieces.

THANK YOU TO THE FOLLOWING SUPPLIERS FOR DONATING MATERIALS USED IN THIS BOOK:

Clothing: Rachel Riley (www.rachelriley.co.uk). **Fabric and textiles:** Clark & Clark; HobbyCraft; Liberty; The Eternal Maker. **Paint and furnishings:** Farrow & Ball; Love Lane Vintage. **Other:** Canon Cameras; The Bubble Shop

Recommended Stockists and Suppliers

CRAFTS/FABRIC SUPPLIERS

Clark & Clark
(High-quality fabrics)
www.clarke-clarke.co.uk

Fabric Rehab
(Funky, retro and modern fabrics)
www.fabricrehab.co.uk

Fred Aldous Ltd
(Art, craft and design supplies)
www.fredaldous.co.uk

HobbyCraft
(Arts and crafts superstore)
www.hobbycraft.co.uk

Husqvarna Viking
(Sewing machine specialists)
www.husqvarnaviking.com

Liberty (department store)
www.liberty.co.uk

The Cotton Patch
(Patchwork & quilting shop)
www.cottonpatch.co.uk

The Eternal Maker
(Imported crafting fabric)
www.eternalmaker.com

The Quilt Room
(Patchwork/quilting specialists)
www.quiltroom.co.uk

FOOD SUPPLIERS

SK Hutchings Butcher
High Street, Partridge Green
West Sussex, RH13 8HU

The Salmon Shop
(Fresh and frozen seafood)
www.thesalmonshop.co.uk

GARDEN

Crocus
(Plants/gardening equipment)
www.crocus.co.uk

Dobies of Devon
(Online plant specialists)
www.dobies.co.uk

Old Barn Nursery and
Garden Centre
(Online plants, trees and shrubs)
www.thegardencentregroup.co.uk

**KITCHENWARE AND
HOMEWARE SUPPLIERS**

Anolon
(Cooking and baking equipment)
www.raymondblancbyanolon.com

Cath Kidston
(Homewares and fabric)
www.cathkidston.co.uk

Diptyque Paris
(Candles and fragrances)
www.diptyqueparis.co.uk

Divertimenti
(Kitchen and tableware)
www.divertimenti.co.uk

John Lewis (department store)
www.johnlewis.com

Joseph Joseph

(Contemporary kitchenware)
www.josephjoseph.com

Kitchen Aid
(Iconic kitchen equipment)
www.kitchenaid.co.uk

Kitchen Craft
(Kitchenware supplier)
www.kitchencraft.co.uk

Laura Ashley
(Home furnishings)
www.lauraashley.com

Lakeland
(Specialist kitchen equipment)
www.lakeland.co.uk

Stellar
www.stellarcookware.co.uk

PAINT AND FURNISHINGS

Farrow & Ball
(Heritage wallpaper and paint;
www.farrow-ball.com);

Love Lane Vintage
(Furniture/china/linen hire)
www.lovelanevintage.co.uk

PARTY SUPPLIERS

The Bubble Shop
www.thebubbleshop.com

Party Pieces
www.partypieces.co.uk

Shop Sweet Lulu
www.shopsweetlulu.com

Index

Thank you to ...

Amanda Preston, my agent, for always believing in me. Amanda Harris, my publisher at Orion, for taking a punt on a complete unknown. Lucie Stericker, the creative director at Orion, for having the best eye in the business – even after being stung by a bee. Aruna Vasudevan, my editor, for being very calm and gentle with a total novice. Nikki Dupin, designer of this beautiful book and my good friend. Keiko Oikawa, my photographer and the sweetest soul I know. Kuo Kang Chen, for your lovely craft illustrations and Nikki Morgan and her male helpers, LOVE you guys! All of you made this experience utterly unforgettable and totally collaborative.

Helena Lang and the team at *Sainsbury's Magazine*; Richard and Sheelagh Eyre; Emma Freud, for writing a foreword that made me cry on a train.

All the people who read my blog and website, without you no publisher would have touched me. Thank you for reading me.

Thank you to my friends, my parents, my family, and Robert's mum, Sue, who helped our little family through Robert's illness as this book was being made. But most of all, thank you to my dear sister Jodie, my darling husband Robert, and my twins Ned and Anaïs, you are my life.